The Bible for Men
Vol. 1
Women Friends
and Male Power

Richard D. Mills

PublishAmerica
Baltimore

Book Illustrations: Mario Cortes; Cover Photography: James Laub; Book Cover Models: Lin Bennett, Maria Elena Martinez, Art Richard, Ian Lombard, Phil Burdick.

First printing

ISBN: 1-4137-6222-0
PUBLISHED BY PUBLISHAMERICA, LLLP
www.publishamerica.com
Baltimore

Printed in the United States of America

The Bible for Men
Vol. 1
Women Friends
and Male Power

Richard D. Mills

TABLE OF CONTENTS

ACKNOWLEDGMENTS

People say that the true measure of friendship is best assessed during those occasions when we most need our friends' assistance and support. If this is true, the creation of this book has only demonstrated and reconfirmed to me that my friends are absolutely the best of the best. In fact, I would match my friends against those of anyone because they simply don't come in any finer quality. I honestly believed early on that I would be able to create this book and have it published without placing any imposition on either of my male or female buddies, but I was deeply mistaken. And how fortunate for me that my friends are who they are, because without them there is virtually no chance this book would exist. Not only have many of my friends stepped up time and again to give me research, editing, content and critiquing support, they have all helped in their own special way to make my life the absolute joy it is to live. So how does a guy properly thank all of the people who have helped him along the way and who have inspired him to be so much more than he would have been without their participation and influence?

The number of people I need to acknowledge for inspiration in the writing of this book are far too numerous to list. There are my closest friends, former girlfriends, current women friends, male buddies, my parents, my siblings, many extended family members, certain petty tyrants who unwittingly motivated me, and so many others. And how does one acknowledge the love, good will, financial resources and personal energies so many have shared and freely given to help me in life's journey? Do I need to give special thanks to everyone I've had meaningful exchanges and interaction with and who have inspired my life? Or, do I just acknowledge a specific number of them like Dr. Patricia Lawrence, Bobbi Atkins and Steve Murray, who set aside their precious time, energies and many of their strong, personal convictions to help challenge me with the contents of this book? Do I just acknowledge Suzanne Roady-Ross for her superlative editing skills that took her years to build as a student and teacher? And how do I best thank Art Richard for being the skilled research veteran he is and for loaning those skills to me?

I doubt that my mother, Dr. Carrol Lee Mills, has any idea of what a tremendous force she has been in stimulating my intellectual curiosity and development, and I am even more fortunate to have had my father, Richard A. Mills, as an equal force in stimulating and challenging my spiritual development. What an incredibly fortunate human being I am to have had the brunt of their collective power working in my favor. I cannot see any possibility of the emotional and spiritual balance that has truly occurred in my life without the combined, sustained and dedicated efforts of them both. And I have never ever, not once in my lifetime, wished or dreamed that I had been parented by any others.

Some of my closets buddies and allies like Stephen Bruce, Joe Bongiorno, Dave Denton, Janice Simmons, Jonathon Grossgold, Barry Snyder, Jordan Chandler, John Dorch, Mark Anderson and Robert Easley have contributed to and inspired this book in ways they cannot even begin to imagine. And then there are long-time friends and companions like Phil Burdick, Lin Bennett and Nancy Nemzek who have made significant contributions by simply being a part of my life and making sure that I am aware of their constant affection and deep abiding regard. A special thank you has to go to my friend and best-selling women's author, Lynn V. Andrews, who truly inspired this particular book by mentoring me and telling me point blank to get off my ass and get it written. This woman has pushed me gently, but powerfully, in ways so subtle, yet so blatant, that I wouldn't know how to explain them.

So let me say thanks, with utmost humility, to everyone I have mentioned here. Your love, struggles, sacrifices and accomplishments have served me in ways I am only now beginning to realize. What a truly fortunate, prosperous, grateful and joyful human being I have become because of you and your influence in my life.

FIRST WORD

"There is one thing stronger than all the armies in the world,
and that is an idea whose time has come."
~ Victor Hugo ~

I am thrilled to have been born male. I genuinely love being a guy and I love everything that goes along with guyness. For me, being born male is a gift from the universe that I feel overwhelmingly blessed to have received. I am also firmly convinced that I had something to do with choosing the gender I happen to be, but I still see it as a blessing, nevertheless, and one that I value beyond measure. And in all honesty, the thing I think I enjoy the most about being male is the connection and relationship it has given me to women— Mother Earth's* other, softer gender creation.*

I think women are absolutely marvelous creatures and I simply cannot get enough of them. I seek out their company; I like their smell; I love the shape and feel of their bodies; I like to catch their gaze; I love to watch them walk by; I enjoy their feminine voices; I love the way they dress; I enjoy their limitless differences in general; and I am especially thrilled when they choose to love me. As I look back over the years, I am in awe of the employment I have taken, the places I have chosen to live, and the educational choices I've

*I chose to capitalize the word *Earth* because it is just my little demonstration of respect and way of honoring the mother of all humankind and the mother of all life on this planet.
**I prefer to refer to women as "the other gender" instead of the "opposite sex" because the word *opposite* implies a form of opposition, and I do *not* feel opposed to women in any way.

made because of my powerful desire to be around women. When, for example, I was living at a popular Southern California beach where women wear clothing that is barely legal and attending the largest university in California where there were more available women than at any other university, I also worked at a large hospital because I couldn't think of any other working environment where there would be more available women for dating. And then, when I would meet a woman with whom I would form a bond, I would find and feel the joy I was so eager to capture. In fact, there are few joys that I would rather experience than the joy I feel when I am in the company of a woman who is happy to love me, as I am, and who is comfortable with letting me know the full extent of her affection.

I don't intend to make this sound as if the connection I have to women is an end-all to being male, but rather one of the most enjoyable parts of being a man I have experienced in this life and world. In writing this book, it is my intention to impart this joy to as many other men as possible, and to help men (and women alike) to learn to see and experience the other gender in a more positive and rewarding light. And although I am educated and experienced in the social science of psychology, this book is a product of my spiritual journeys and convictions and is in no way intended to be a work of psychological theory and rhetoric.

Western societies, along with many others, have evolved from a long history of prearranged unions to those of individual romantic choice. And even though our history of romance is relatively new and has been nowhere near as long-lived and enduring as the traditional arrangement process, the moment has come when evolution of the romantic notion to the stronger foundation of friendship bonding has become of paramount importance.

I must, however, give a very stern warning at this point to the readers who choose to read through the next few pages and cross over the threshold of Chapter One; it is most certainly my intention to aggressively challenge many commonly held concepts and beliefs about coupling, marrying and romancing that the general population currently views as steadfast and unalterable truisms. And it is also my purpose to point out some of the origins and pitfalls of common coupling practices and beliefs that some people may experience as distressing.

The Bible For Men is intended to be the new handbook for the ever-growing audience of men: primarily single, but also married, separated, or disenfranchised, for whatever reason, by the current system of coupling and marriage. And this book is no way intended to be an indictment of quality marital unions nor an excuse for men to shirk their moral obligations, responsibilities and commitments within the framework of the marriage agreement. There is an untold enormity of joy, reward and growth to be achieved from both the marriage and romance experience. But as research, modern trends and personal experience are indicating, it is very difficult and highly improbable to build a dependable and enduring other-gender relationship solely upon the shaky, short-term foundation provided by the current form of marriage and romance. So if creating desirable, solid, dependable and enduring other-gender relationships are important to men, we need to dramatically shift our focus and dreams to the more pragmatic, consistent and permanent cornerstone concepts of friendship-bonding.

Women are wonderful creatures who make the experience of life a very enjoyable journey if we let them. But there are many single men who see them as the source of their wounds and as alien creatures who come from a place that is far beyond the orbit of Venus. Males who observed and experienced relationship building before the feminist movement of the 1960s and 1970s are often confused by the opposing sets of standards they witnessed while living through two different eras. And males who were born during or after the 1960s and 1970s are often confused by the tacit social acceptance that men are naturally born as immoral animals who must now be rehabilitated by the politically correct. Consequently, it is imperative that these men learn to become friends with women before they can consider any other aspects of relationship-bonding. Then there are other men who enjoy their contact with women, but who prefer to place the bulk of their focus on other aspects of life such as career, adventure and travel. So these men need to center their efforts with women on the power and benefits of friendship-bonding as well.

In Part I of *The Bible For Men*, we will glance briefly backward and will view the historical path we men have taken to arrive in the world of relationships as we know them today. It is imperative to see how we have created our own conditions in order to take full responsibility for them. And not until we do take full personal responsibility are we able to change course once again and deliberately create new, more suitable, rewarding, and satisfying relationship conditions for our individual futures.

In Part II we will begin to look at the specific roadmaps necessary for changing our course yet again. Because believe it or not, there are worlds upon worlds out there that are different from the one we live in now—and worlds where there are endless numbers of women who are just waiting to meet men like us. So whatever types of relationships we have been looking to find and have been fantasizing about since the beginning of our adolescent sexual development, we need to take heart because they are already in existence and are simply waiting for our arrival. To achieve them we simply need to reclaim our male power and be willing to have the women and relationships that we truly want and absolutely deserve to have.

> *"Give a man a fish and you feed him for a day;*
> *teach a man to fish*
> *and you feed him for a lifetime."*
> *~ Lao Tzu ~*

PART ONE:
THE OLD TESTAMENT

EVOLVING FROM ARRANGED COUPLING TO THE INDIVIDUAL CHOICE OF ROMANCE

A Woman's Rule of Thumb:
"If it has tires or testicles, you're going to have trouble with it."
~ Anonymous ~

It doesn't really matter exactly what the ideal relationship looks like to the individual person per se, as long as he can form some basic concept and feeling for it. Then, as his personal power allows and grows from doggedly adhering to the precepts set forth in this *Bible For Men*, he can learn to withstand the impact of letting go of the old and entering the new. So the challenge is to learn how to dream a new dream, and then with great facility, turn and step directly into it.

Learning to turn and face the boundaries of the world, then step across those boundaries into an entirely new existence, takes the fortitude of a strong, independent, well-developed constitution. Just imagine, for example, that a person decides to quit his job today and become self-employed tomorrow, or that he throws away his secure form of income to become an artist, an actor, or do something entirely new? Where would the money and resources come from to pay the bills, sustain his lifestyle, or even improve it? Although most of us would take a good deal of time and planning to accomplish such a maneuver, the result is still the same; the more secure and familiar world of a regular paycheck and financial security is gone. And the more secure world is replaced by the uncertain world of self-employment with no guarantees. So how do we begin to make such a dramatic transition in our affairs with women?

In this bible, the first step is to understand how we achieved the world that we now perceive. And although this is the only world that most of us have known, we certainly didn't arrive here overnight. So let us begin by taking a look at how we made the journey to arrive in the current world of social gender awareness.

"Great things are not done by impulse,
but by a series of small things brought together."
~ Vincent van Gogh ~

1
Book One:
GENESIS OF THE DEAL

"It is not the strongest of the species that survive,
nor the most intelligent,
but the one most responsive to change."
~ Charles Darwin ~

In the beginning, it was the male who created "The Deal," which is a term my buddy Juan uses to describe the process that men and women undertake when they first meet and are attempting to develop an intimate relationship. Juan dislikes our current version of The Deal because he feels strongly that he and other males alike have been extorted and held hostage by this process for the past several decades, and that it puts the male gender at a total disadvantage when trying to form physically intimate compacts with potential lovers. In theory, I would have to completely agree with my long-term buddy on this overall premise, but I am certainly not as militant about it as he is. Every chance Juan gets he admonishes his male friends and acquaintances to reject this common, unholy, blasphemous and self-destructive practice by being willing to forgo any sexual rewards it may bring, in either the short or the long run. In fact, he lives to debunk The Deal and loves to debate it with women too, especially any opinionated women

17

who are game enough to take him on.

Everyone knows that from the very first moment we start dating we initiate either a subtle or not so subtle negotiation process. Across the majority of species, Mother Nature and evolution have arranged it so males generally want immediate access to the females' bodies and females want to get the best deal they can get for this access before giving males the inevitable admission rights that they require and demand.

"While your friend holds you affectionately by both your hands
you are safe, for you can watch both his."
~ Ambrose Bierce ~

Because of historical human rituals, our worldwide social courtship practices have created an axiom of perception where we perceive sexual activity as a woman giving up merchandise that is very valuable and precious to her, while a man is gaining merchandise of great value that inherently belongs to someone else. To illustrate this belief system one only needs to scan the endless pages of romantic literature and modern film productions for references by poets, pundits, writers, religious-minded believers, and a host of others who have consistently referred to a woman's sexuality as "a flower" (which includes many varieties); "her blossom," and "her most valued, private, and vulnerable possession." Remember high school? The girls were always on guard and we guys were always trying to get our hands on them and our penises into them. But not, of course, until the girls got the agreements or best deals they thought they could get, which for most meant declarations of love and promises of marriage.

"Woman begins by resisting a man's advances
and ends by blocking his retreat."
~ Oscar Wilde ~

While an undergraduate and graduate student of psychology at California State University Long Beach, I had the opportunity to spend some valuable time working as a counselor. In fact, I even supervised a nonprofit clinic for a short time that specializes in family planning and family counseling. Since a large part of my counseling duties revolved around the task of counseling couples who sought help for their relationship woes, it seemed to me that it would be a smart move to become a student of relationship and marital history. So I read everybody I could find in those days, most notably Wayne Dyer, Nathaniel Brandon, Herb Goldberg, Helen Fisher, Mary Batten, Marilyn Ferguson and Carl Jung, among numerous others, and as a result, I was able to see how The Deal took form and evolved over many millennia.

Apparently, the concept of marriage began during the agricultural revolution around 8000 BC, which would now make it about ten thousand years old. As some hunters and gatherers learned that they could stay in one place and grow food, the need for migration and/or "hunting and gathering" became less important while the more pragmatic need for a nuclear family became paramount. When a farmer would plant his crops and then harvest them, he would pile them in a single location that was often left unguarded so he could return to his fields and continue to work. While he was away from his food stashes, the neighboring hunters and gatherers would come upon his harvest and pilfer them. So to counter these acts of thievery he and his fellow farmers began to form communities where each member would take his turn staying behind to provide security and guard the community's crops while the others went to their fields to continue their work. Although this is clearly a simplified version of agricultural history, the need for security and teamwork resulted in the formation of numerous communities where civilization was born. But since it was necessary for some farmers to stay behind to guard the harvest and homes of others, there was no one else to work in their fields, to take care of their homes, and tend to their livestock. And a farmer's wealth and livelihood depended a great deal on someone tending his crops and livestock.

The more farmhands a farmer had, the more wealth and security he could generate, and this type of world economy ruled supreme for thousands of years. Of course, the farmer couldn't just go out and hire anyone because he needed to pay them and he needed farmhands who would be loyal and accountable to him. So he decided to capitalize on the resources and methods most expedient to him and therefore set out to procreate numerous sons. To have sons, however, he needed women, and the best way to acquire them was to buy them from his neighbors. Pretty ingenious maneuver if you ask me, but I doubt that Mr. and Mrs. Jackson, who lived next door to my family while I was growing up in Topeka, Kansas, would have taken it too well if I would have offered them some goats and sheep for one of their daughters. Mr. Jackson did love my father's German Shepard police dog named Caesar, but unfortunately Caesar belonged to the city police department and wasn't mine to bargain with. In any event, *arranged marriage* was conceived ten thousand years ago along with civilization, and the method of consummation all of those past thousands of years has been the transaction we now know as "The Deal."

ADAM AND EVE

M. CORTES

According to many anthropologists and sociologists the practice of *arranged marriage* is still more common and widely used in the world's numerous societies than is the romantic selection process that most of us prefer in the Western world. So the ancient form of matchmaking and haggling for one's bride is still alive and well throughout the globe. In many of these societies, the only way to increase the social and economic standing of one's family is to marry off the daughters to suitors from families with more wealth and higher social standing than those of their own. Otherwise, there is virtually no chance of upward mobility and increased economic rewards in their future. Eventually, the practice of buying a wife changed in many of these societies to the initial investment being made by the bride's family. In this form of The

Deal the wife's family buys their way into the groom's family with a dowry that first has to be negotiated like any other business transaction. And although it costs the bride's family at first, it is still the long-term responsibility of the groom and his family to clothe, house and feed their new female property from then on, and in some cases be charitable over the long-term to her family of origin as well. In these societies, the art of The Deal is vital to family survival and therefore of major significance and importance to the very foundations of the society as a whole. So The Deal, which is an ancient business transaction, permeates all aspects of their lives that includes familial, social, political and religious.

Even to this day there are numerous forms of *arranged marriage* that have nothing to do with the concepts of love and romance as we know them in the Western world. In Northern India, for example, there is an area where children as young as ten, eleven, and twelve are married off to spouses of equal age in elaborate ceremonies with grand fanfare. Although the practice is technically illegal according to the country's laws, it is still openly and widely practiced in this region because of the strong and durable moral, social and religious beliefs that permeate this specific society. Because the children are so young when they marry they continue to remain at home with their parents and are encouraged to carry on their lives as children until the age of sixteen, when they go to live with their handpicked spouse. But even then they have had almost no contact with their spouse and absolutely no romance or love is involved in the process. If they learn to become friends once they have begun to live together there is a good chance that love will eventually grow between them, but there is no guarantee this love will ever occur.

"Marriage: putting one's hand into a bag of snakes
on the chance of drawing out an eel."
~ Leonardo da Vinci ~

In additional forms of *arranged marriage* that have evolved in the larger cities of the East, Middle East, and other parts of the world including the Western world, some choice is involved. In these situations the potential bride and groom are usually allowed to meet each other on one occasion, but only with members of both families present to oversee the conference. In some cases the couples are allowed to talk in private for only a few minutes to discuss future aspirations, but they most often have to make up their minds to marry or not from these brief and mostly supervised encounters. Then, the families make all of the arrangements and several weeks or several months later the couple is married without ever having had any further contact with one another. Again, love is almost never discussed and neither love nor romance takes any part in the process. If the couple is fortunate enough to be left alone for a brief and private discussion, the conversation usually covers very practical concerns about education, career, and family expectations. But love, romance, and passion play virtually no role in the process of selecting a mate and lifetime partner.

For most of us in the Western world and contemporary world of romance, it would be unthinkable to select a mate for whom we felt no passion, either physically or emotionally. And the majority of us wouldn't even consider the possibility of creating a family with someone who had never shared her ideas and philosophies about child rearing, finances, general domestic responsibilities, etc. So how could people survive a lifetime of marriage with someone they didn't even know when they wed them?

The now-common practice of romantic unions as we know them in the contemporary world is roughly one hundred fifty years old. Compared to the ten thousand-year history of the arrangement concept, we are still pretty much novices when it comes to individual choice. Just look at what happened only five hundred years ago to those poor irrational lovers, Romeo and Juliet, when they tried to usurp the family's traditional, tried and proven arrangement system for one of romance. Talk about a futile effort and complete disaster—their ill-fated attempt cost them their lives. But we shouldn't try to kid ourselves about the change from their time to our own, because The Deal is still alive and well in our modern methods, and it has gleefully made the transition from arranged unions to the ones we now create through romantic, individual choice. The primary difference, of course, is that it has only changed its appearance and today's men and women tend do their own wheeling and dealing for sex and love.

The Deal is a product of the merchant mind no matter how we attempt to describe it or justify its practice. No matter what our clergymen, grandmothers, teachers, aunties, best friends, or society at large have told us, the importance and value of female virginity was never about virtue, but was rather a product of The Deal and of getting the best terms possible. Male religious leaders supported and encouraged the arrangement process throughout the centuries and made virginity a religious issue to support and serve the process of The Deal. And the bottom line has been that the less used the woman is the more value she often has to potential male suitors, an ancient concept that has carried over to our contemporary world of romance as well. Consider The Deal-making process and concept of virtue in a country like Afghanistan and think of negotiating for a bride there. If she is untouched, her value is top of the scale. If she is used, even by rape, she is either abandoned or killed by the males in her family. If she's really lucky, to be rid of her the family may give her away to someone who doesn't have the wherewithal to get anyone else. Why should the family feed, clothe and house her when she has no market value, or any other practical value for that matter, and has only become an expensive consumer and financial liability?

Fortunately for the more forward and contemporary thinking guys, however, there are a few hundred million marvelous, intelligent, educated, attractive, professional, highly available women in the modern world who see themselves as valuable, no matter how many men they've been with. And I for one am absolutely thrilled to know that there may be a billion or two of them who exist.

"God created sex. Priests created marriage."
~ Voltaire ~

2

Book Two:
EXODUS OF
THE OLD DEAL

"Life is a romantic business,
but you have to make the romance."
~ Oliver Wendell Holmes ~

The antecedents and harbingers of today's individual romantic selection process appeared on the scene about five hundred years ago with Shakespeare and the poetic Troubadours. Coupling was still an arranged affair for sure, but the idea of romantic partnering was beginning to gain a strong foothold and the foundations of today's romantic "hooking up" process were laid. Getting laid also became the favorite social pastime for female aristocrats who were busy taking seductive Troubadours and others as lovers, and often to the man's peril when caught by wealthy and powerful husbands. But love affairs were growing in popularity and practice during this time period, and finding and maintaining romantic partnerships became a focus of those with the opportunity and the means to indulge themselves.

After "the colonies" in America won their independence from their European lords, a new liberalism became freer to set in with democracy. This new liberalism opened the door for older bachelors, spinsters, widows, and widowers to start selecting their mates through personal preferences, but younger people still had to have the family's blessing and permission. During the mid and late 1800s, more and more sons and daughters were using the personal freedom brought about by democracy and independence from the Old World to claim their individual right to choose their own mates. As democracy spread throughout the Western world, so did individual choice, and it has since flowed rapidly into numerous societies that were and are non-democratic. Eventually, it took the shape that we know today.

Researchers report that education and information in the more traditional societies is now causing a major decline in *arranged marriages*. It appears that the younger generation is learning about contraceptives and the scientific explanations for religious myths and other taboos once used as justification for specific behaviors and practices. So is it any wonder that religious leaders have so often shunned and ridiculed education and theological study outside of their own belief systems?

Nowadays, there are countless self-help and relationship books that tell us how to build healthy and fulfilling unions based on romantic principles. A fairly well-known version that hit the shelves in the mid to late 1990s is one of those books that my male friends just love to hate: *The Rules*, which depicts a passing era that still flourished and had implicit acceptance through the 1950s. If anyone has not read this book or heard of it, the nicest thing I can say is that it is nothing more than a set of unfriendly guidelines for scheming wannabe wives who are comfortable with the notion of manipulating mindless men into marrying them. Since its precepts are built upon the old-fashioned notions of courtly romance that lead inevitably to marriage, the book was widely accepted and the authors were featured on numerous news programs and talk shows. Frankly, the book is annoying to me because it is full of machinations designed to negotiate a Deal that has nothing to do with friendship or integrity. For example, here are a few of the "Rules" the authors instruct women to follow:

- Never talk to a man first and don't ask him to dance.
- Never meet a man half-way or go Dutch on a date.
- Don't call him and only rarely return his calls.
- Never agree to a Saturday night date after Wednesday.
- Always end dates and phone calls first.
- Never ever break the rules.

I can just see myself dating a woman who follows rules like these. Well, this is not true, because it is highly unlikely that I would have enough in common with a rules girl to date her. So it would probably go something like this:

It's Thursday Evening:

The Phone Rings: Ring, ring, ring.

Sally: "Hello?"

Me: "Hey cutie, I got home earlier from my business trip than I expected, and I figured that you and I should hook up Saturday, go for a nice dinner, see a movie, and have wild erotic sex, not necessarily in that order."

Sally: "Oh, I am sorry, Richard, as much as I would enjoy seeing you and even though I am completely available and horny as hell, I simply cannot accept a date with you for Saturday."

Me: "Oh, is that so? Well, how about Sunday then? I'm flexible!"

Sally: "I'm sorry, Sunday won't do either. You'll have to call me by Wednesday of next week if you would like to see me the following weekend."

Me: "Oh, is that a rule or something?"

Sally: "Why yes, I am a 'Rules Girl', you know, and we never ever break the rules for any reason."

Me: "A 'Rules Girl', huh?"

Sally: "Absolutely! So I have to assume that you don't care about spontaneity and common friendship courtesies and that playing on your predatory male instincts will be enough to hook you forever."

Me: "And if it is not?"

Sally: "Well, as I said, a 'Rules Girl' can never break the rules."

Me: "You're pulling my leg, right?"

Sally: "Oh no, you're lucky I even answered the phone because it is after Wednesday and I have caller ID, so I knew it was you."

Me: "Wow, that's very interesting to say the least, but I have a rule of thumb I follow too."

Sally: "Oh, you do?"

Me: "Yep, I don't do 'Rules Girls', nor do I follow the rules they establish."

Sally: "But you must if we are to have a relationship."

Me: "Oh, yeah? And how long do you think your women friends would stay around if you treated them like this?"

Like it or not, the 1960s changed our lives and society forever. It was the time when women became sexual beings who had choices of their own and it was the beginning of an era when competing in a man's world was no longer taboo. Women like my mother, Dr. Carrol Lee Mills, wore T-shirts that said, "A woman's place is in the House, and the Senate." And she pounded it into me that a woman's body was her own and that no one had ownership rights to it but herself.

My mother was a teenager when I was born, so she finished high school and went to college to become a psychologist while my older sister Vicky and I were trying to grow up. She certainly wasn't a radical feminist by any interpretation that I am aware of, but she hated the fact that the older, stronger, and more powerfully outspoken matriarchs in her family berated her for working and going to school instead of staying home to rear her children. The fact is, my young father usually worked two and three jobs at a time, but still didn't produce enough income for us to survive on without my mother's full-time financial contributions. And when she eventually earned her Ph.D., the final insult came in the form of congratulatory letters and cards from the matriarchs of her family who addressed them to "Mrs. Richard Mills" instead of to "Dr. Carrol Lee Mills." But eventually, about ten years later, the matriarchs had to change their tune when my parents divorced and my mother was able to maintain her hard-earned, upper-middle class lifestyle on her own and immediately purchase her own nice home.

> *"If we are to achieve a richer culture,*
> *rich in contrasting values,*
> *we must recognize the whole gamut of human potentialities,*
> *and so weave a less arbitrary social fabric,*
> *one in which each diverse gift*
> *will find a fitting place."*
> ~ *Margaret Mead* ~

Since the 1960s and 1970s there has been a mini-revival of sorts and some of the customary dating courtesies and rituals of the pre-1960s have been reestablished. But all in all, we live in an entirely different world where women and men are expected to make their own choices and follow their own hearts when it comes to love and coupling. And the primary guide to coupling that most people in this world follow is the *Spirit of Romance*, but I think the *God of Romance* has become a more fitting and accurate name than "spirit." Although men were largely responsible for the proliferation of romance in the beginning, we now live in a society where the expectation and demand for it is fueled primarily by women. Just scroll through some of the tens of thousands of personal ads posted on the Internet to see what I mean. The men's profiles rarely refer to it, but nearly every single one of the women's narratives is either titled with or refers to romance. Here are just a very few that I've seen:

"Romantic Lady Looking For Romantic Gent"

"I just love to be romanced, don't you?"

"Only Romantic Men Need Apply"

"Must be romantic"

"Romance a must"

"Hooked on romance"

"Loves romantic evenings out"

"Loves romantic dinners and long romantic walks on the beach"

"I'm a die hard romantic"

"I'm a romantic at heart"

"Loves romance in all forms"

"Likes romantic evenings in front of the fireplace"

"Seeking Romance"

"I believe in romance"

"Tired of living without romance"

"Loves flowers and other romantic gifts"

"Mother of grown children seeks romance"

"Addicted to romance, need injection"

"If you're not romantic, don't bother contacting me"

Romance has become such an important and popular god that we have named days for it like Valentine's Day and we have developed a multibillion-dollar economy that flourishes on it with endless romance novels, multimillion dollar movie productions, a chocolate and candy industry, romantic hotels, cruises, florists, etc. As a powerful social force it is nearly impossible to escape romance or find anyone in our modern world who doesn't practice some form of it at least occasionally. So is there any wonder that I would refer to it as a god?

> *"The life of man is the true romance, which when it is valiantly conducted, will yield the imagination a higher joy than any fiction."*
> *~ Ralph Waldo Emerson ~*

3

Book Three:
THE NUMBERS
OF SPIRITS

"You can chain me,
you can torture me,
you can even destroy this body,
but you will never imprison my mind."
~ Mahatma Gandhi ~

It may seem odd to some, but through my spiritual growth I have developed the ability to see the spirits of our world. I see them as living beings, or fields of energy, with whom I can converse. They appear daily through life experience or I can usually summon them when it is necessary. In fact, I run into the spirit of romantic love on a regular basis these days, but he has a different impact on me than he once did. We know each other pretty well and I used to think I had to let him run my affairs with women. But we've created a different kind of working relationship these days and I use him as a consultant to advise me when I think it is necessary. Some of us may know this spirit as female and others may know it as male. I only call it a "he" because of my own experience with it and the lack of a more appropriate word. We have given many names and faces to this spirit and it has survived on the earth for a number of centuries now. Some may know it as Venus or Aphrodite, others may know it as Cupid or Eros, and still others may know it in the form of Sirens and Nymphs. In any event, we humans have a serious habit of personifying the beings that most of us know only as human attributes and emotions. So, it is important to modify the history lesson a little in this chapter and clarify something a bit ethereal and mythical that I will be dealing with throughout the remainder of this book.

If one really thinks about it, emotional responses like hate, passion, fear, joy, greed, lust, jealousy, and other such traits were here in the world long before we were born, and will likely be here long after we have died. Because of recorded history, we can be pretty sure these entities have been living for thousands and perhaps tens of thousands of years among humans. And the key operative words here are *entities* and *living* because these spirits certainly have a life of their own.

"What's that you say, Richard? They are alive?"

Well sure, why not?

Hate feeds off of people's energy, just as we feed off of vegetables, fruits, meats and breads. Without our energy, how would emotions like hate and love survive? We call the spirit of giving Santa Claus and the spirit of death the Grim Reaper, and we have given them human form and traits. Heck, Santa Claus even has a house, a wife, full-time employees, flying pets, and his own trademark clothing. And as long as we believe in him and give him life, he lives! Each year I see him on numerous television shows, in movies, in stores, and his image plastered all over homes, cities and retail outlets.

The Romans and Greeks called these spirits or entities "gods," and good or bad, gave them names like Zeus, Pan, Hera, Jupiter, Juno, Cupid, Eros, Hades and Aphrodite. The Christian Bible refers to the more negative entities as "demons," and to the positive entities as "angels," while the Koran refers to the negatives as "Infidels." The Carlos Castaneda books refers to all of them neutrally as "Inorganic Beings," which is the term that I prefer. But regardless of the names that human kind has given them, we know that we've given them life and that we keep them alive in our world with our human energy. We do not let our *social minds* think in these terms generally because we have been taught not to, but once we do we can see them for what they are, which are fields of energy with limited awareness that feed off of human beings to stay alive.

> *"The artist alone sees spirits.*
> *But after he has told of their appearing to him, everybody sees them."*
> *~ Johann Wolfgang von Goethe ~*

Just imagine Elsie the cow figuring out that ranchers only raised her to make babies so we humans can eat them. I can just see her going from barnyard to barnyard, pasture to pasture, and range to range holding freedom rallies and moo-ins in an effort to spread the word and let her fellow cows know that they have been had. Well, in a vein similar to Elsie and her rancher/breeder, these entities do the same with us. Take the spirit of bigotry, for example. In the movie *Jungle Fever* by Spike Lee, a girl of Italian heritage (Annabella Sciorra) has an affair with a married man of African heritage (Wesley Snipes). Even though the girl's family is super racist and she was reared in this bigoted environment, the spirit of bigotry has never had reason to harm her, up until this point anyway. But once Señor Bigotry finds out that she has been ignoring his rules and is seeing a black man, he decides to sic her father and brothers on her and they beat her to a bloody pulp. So for several agonizing hours the spirit of bigotry receives so much human energy that it is able to take over the physical form of the father and brothers to inflict great bodily harm on the gullible, young, female heretic. While watching the movie I could easily see what was coming her way, so why didn't she see it and run like hell?

The Christian Bible has a story about Jesus and his friend Mary Magdalene and how he exorcized seven demons from her. What he actually did with her cooperation was to move her assemblage point, or her point of perception, to a place where she could see these "demons" for herself and as they really are. Once this was accomplished it was just a matter of no longer feeding them until they fled to greener pastures. And I would argue that hate is probably the most likely candidate for the entity that we know as the Satan personified. Along with his right hand general that we've named intolerance, hate is the extreme opposite pole of love, and operates from the darkness and opposes everything that is in the light. When people go to the town square to protest against the demonstrations of hate groups like the Ku Klux Klan, they are only adding their energy to the food that hate lives upon. Hate thrives on the feud between these groups because there is no "positive" hate. Think about it; if no one ever witnessed a hate group's demonstration, what purpose would there be for them to have one?

Just like the spirits of hate and love, the spirits of romance and marriage have a life of their own and a powerful presence in our world. It is such a powerful presence that my buddy Samuel also refers to the spirit of marriage as the "marriage god." He refers to it as a "god" because he is fully aware of its ten thousand-year rule over the human species, the power it has accumulated over this vast amount of time, its multibillion-dollar industry revenue throughout the world, and the ramifications of anyone disregarding its dictates. Not to mention the fact that Samuel's last divorce settlement and act of marital heresy cost him several hundreds of thousands of dollars in hard-earned cash and real estate holdings.

Our world is so ruled by the marriage god that magazines, wedding chapels, books, fairy tales, bridal shows, and entire social structures are built on its ideology. I heard a figure last year about how much of the Unites States' national product comes from the wedding industry and it was in the tens, if not hundreds of billions of dollars and may very well surpass the trillion-dollar mark one day. Even the majority of our leading relationship gurus, experts and authors admonish women to quickly "run away" from men who are not serious about marrying them, as if these men are malevolent social pariahs.

Because I so often run into the marriage and romance gods, I decided to invite them to sit down with me for a book interview. Really! I have random conversations with them both off and on these days, so I thought, why not invite them to participate in this book? Although any one of us can see these entities and can communicate with them any time we choose, most of us do not see them and converse with them as I do. Instead, we listen only to what we are taught both overtly and subtly about them, and then we let them whisper their wishes in our ears until they are displeased and then start shouting or attacking. And if anyone does not believe they can shout or attack, just try to walk out on marriage, or try to change its rules and have affairs, or just try to go away without one's spouse on a long-term vacation without the marriage god's permission. A person who tries any of these maneuvers will have a whole boatload of family members pissed at him and a divorce attorney trying to take him for every dime he is worth. The marriage god is a powerful being for people who feed and believe in it, and its rule is formidable to say the very least.

"There was something awesome in the thought of the solitary mortal standing by the open window and summoning in from the gloom outside the spirits of the netherworld."
~ Sir Arthur Conan Doyle ~

Because I have no interest in being married, the marriage god can be a little withholding and apprehensive with me at times, but she does make a great advisor and she likes to play golf, so I can tap into her knowledge and counsel on the golf course from time to time. The romance god and I have fun together because he knows that I see him for what he is and enjoy his company anyway, especially when he bails me out of the jams I can create for myself with women. Even though I don't really give him the power that most people do, we still remain on very friendly terms and he has become one of my allies, so he gladly accepted my interview offer. I explained to both of these entities that it would be much better if they decided to represent themselves and their own points of view instead of letting me do it for them. I also did my best to convince them both that this book would probably sell quite well and reach millions of readers, so they warmly agreed to do the interview. Both Romance and Marriage are very savvy when it comes to the business of generating revenue.

The first time we met we did so at Cinnamon Productions on Main Street in Seal Beach, California, which is my favorite coffee house. And although I didn't realize it at the time, word spread rapidly throughout the spirit world that a big powwow was occurring.

Me: "Hey guys, thanks for doing the interview. I am sure your fans will appreciate hearing directly from you."

Romance: (Smiling broadly) "It's a pleasure, Richard. As you already know, I have billions of fans and followers, so I am always happy to communicate with them and give them encouragement."

We both look at Marriage and wait for a response. She is brunette today, looks fifty-something at first glance and like a modern grandmother, but when I watch her more closely the full weight of her longevity becomes apparent. Ancient or not, she moves and acts like a much younger and more powerful woman than her years would suggest. She looks a little tired, deep in thought, and as if she has some important concern. Finally Romance, who looks like a handsome, twenty-something male who is tall, dark, muscular and fit, gives her a nudge with an elbow and finally gets Marriage to snap out of her solitude.

Marriage: "I was thinking of how this book you are working on might affect the people you work with, Richard."

Me: "Yes, I have thought of that as well."

Marriage: "You work very hard to strengthen the family support and bonds for the troubled kids who are at the institutions where you consult, yet you are giving very unusual advice to single people and to those who might already be parents."

Me: "I agree, but I don't see any real conflict of interest if people don't take my advice out of context. My real purpose is to strengthen relationships, not to harm them."

Marriage: "Some people, especially women, might take your message to be a little anti-marriage, you know?"

Me: "I guess any change worth pursuing will cause some controversy. But marriage as we've known it is really troubled, so I think it is more important for men and women to learn to be friends than it is to try to keep our same outdated ideas and practices of marriage intact."

Romance: "Sounds reasonable to me."

Marriage: "I guess that building healthier relationships is really what is most important."

Romance: (Smiling broadly) "Now that's the spirit! No pun intended." (He has a devious grin and gives Marriage another playful nudge.)

Me: (Realizing Marriage is concerned about her image these days) "So tell me, Marriage, how does it feel to have lived so long?"

Marriage: "Well, I am a little slower these days. And as a result the men and women in the Western world are waiting longer to get hitched. As you know, the average age of marriage goes up with each passing year."

Me: "So how does that make you feel?"

Marriage: "It makes me feel old! (She laughs) But I am doing much better in the societies where marriage is still an arranged affair." (She gives Romance a patronizing look of 'no thanks to you'.)

Romance: (Shrugging his shoulders in mock innocence) "Hey, I never said that people should wait to get married, so don't blame me for your disappointments. I bring them to your altars all the time."

"Never say that marriage has more of joy than pain."
~ Euripides ~

Marriage: (Playfully sarcastic, but with intent) "Well, everyone knows the romance goes out of the relationship once a couple has been married for a while, so it sure isn't in your best interest to hurry them!"

Romance: (Completely unruffled) "Well, I don't actively try to slow them down, but I do prefer it when the romance lasts a bit longer. And I can't help it if romance lasts longer with unmarried couples than it does with married couples."

Me: "Yeah, how about that? The divorce rate is higher for couples who live together before they get married, too."

Marriage: "Yes, that's true, but most of them will probably get married a few more times anyway. And in common law states, marriage is achieved by minor acts of cohabitation."

Me: "So why are couples more likely to split if they marry after living together for a few years?"

Romance: "Easy, because marriage started out as a property and ownership type of arrangement and people still act this way. Once live-in lovers get married it is not as easy to end the relationship, so they begin to forget the everyday courtesies of friendship that once held the cohabitation together. They just stop trying so hard and figure they actually belong to one another now, so what's the big deal? When this happens I split the scene pretty fast because I can always see what's coming next."

Marriage: (Very matter-of-fact and gesturing towards Romance with her thumb) "I was doing fine on my own before Mr. Romance here came along and altered things. A few hundred years after he showed up everything became distorted and people wanted passion and infatuation, so arranged marriages started going down hill. With arranged marriage, people married early and there was no divorce or way out, except death, but that didn't really change anything either, because the widow or widower would just remarry someone else. And even though people think they die and leave the world forever, I've got news for them."

Me: (Looking at Romance) "Yeah? How did you get such a strong foothold in this world anyway? Arranged marriage had a monopoly on the world for ten thousand years, from the beginning of civilization, then all of a sudden you showed up. How the hell did you do that?"

Romance: (Looking smug)

Marriage: "Go on, tell 'em."

Romance: "Well, I've been around longer than you may think, but it was like this. I just happened to be looking around and becoming aware of a strange new world when I overheard several people saying silent prayers and making wishes."

Me: "Wait! You can hear people's thoughts and wishes?"

Romance: "Sort of. It actually has more to do with their energy signatures. I can recognize my own food just like you humans recognize yours. I can smell it, taste it, and know exactly when it is properly prepared and ready for consumption. It has been these thoughts, dreams and wishes that gave me birth and that keeps me alive, and there were so many people in this world who wished and prayed for the ability to choose their mates for themselves that I had no trouble getting the energy I needed to grow. I had thousands of fans almost overnight and those turned into millions and then billions in no time. At first there was tremendous resistance, of course, especially from the religious sector and governments. You know how religious leaders and politicians hate change. They literally ostracized, threatened, tortured, intimidated, and killed the people who wanted to choose their mates for romantic reasons, but eventually I managed to win over many of the dogmatic authorities too, so I was able to grow exponentially in a relatively short amount of time. Once I convinced the authorities they could get more sex if they would just chill out and go along with my program, I had them eating out of my hand. That's when the Romans and the Greeks started to personify me and gave me names, a history, and prominent standing in their societies."

Me: "You know that many of the Christians and other religious followers think that the Romans and Greeks really viewed you as one of their gods."

Romance: "Well, in a way I suppose they did, but they really only referred to me as a god because they realized how much importance the world was starting to give me and how people let me run their lives. I was able and am still able to get billions of people to do my bidding without them even realizing that I am putting them up to it. The same thing is true of all of the other gods they personified and named. They really only believed in one higher power and dominant god like Zeus, but they called us gods and minor gods too because of the powerful influence we had over their civilization and so many lives."

Marriage: (Looking at Romance) "I can still control the masses in spite of you, though, once enough time has passed by in their relationships. If romance leaves before the couple ties the knot, then it is likely they won't ever marry one another. But whenever a couple doesn't marry due to the absence of romance, they eventually get new partners and then they marry. So eventually, they always come back to me, time and time again, even though the romance is almost always lost. No matter how crummy a marriage is or how badly it ends, they almost always come back to me and do it again."

Me: "You certainly have a vast industry and lots of financial resources at your disposal to sell yourself."

Marriage: (Pointing at Romance) "Yes, we both do. It's the money we can generate and the power it buys that keeps us alive and powerful. The millions upon millions of people in the marriage business help to keep us alive by promoting and advertising us. Business people spend billions of dollars each year to get people to marry and then to use their products and services when they do. Even the churches and governments do the same thing."

Me: "So neither one of you is worried about the gay people's demand to have legally recognized marriage rights?"

Marriage & Romance: (In unison) "No way!"

Marriage: "Marriage is marriage. I can't imagine why the gay and lesbian communities want to be like the rest of the world, except for the financial benefits of course, but who cares? As long as they pay me due homage, I don't give a hoot what gender they are. In fact, I was thinking seriously about bringing those smug politicians and religious leaders down a few pegs who think marriage is only for them and other heteros. But in the end, they won't matter much because same-sex unions are going to be legally recognized, sooner or later, and those critics will only end up as historical figures who clung to discriminatory policies and tried to fight tolerance and social progress. (Shaking her head) Remember the religious leaders who tried to suppress Copernicus and Galileo? If it were left up to those clowns everyone would still think the earth is flat and at the center of the solar system, not to mention the universe!"

Me: "This reminds me of the photos I've seen from the early 1900s, where women are picketing the beaches because other women are wearing bathing suits that reveal their legs from the knee or thigh down. The picket signs all claim that revealing their bare knees and lower legs will be the doom of society and nothing but evil and damnation will come of it. But I can't imagine anyone wanting to take our society back to the practices and social taboos of that era."

Romance: (Smiling) "Here, here!" Same-sex unions often have all the romantic notions that heteros have, so bring 'em on! Besides, there are more than twenty-five million gay people in the U.S. alone with a purchasing power of more than one-half trillion dollars, so the marriage industry is just gnawing at the bit to let them join in the fun."

Me: "So what about Friendship?"

Marriage: (Raises her eyebrows questioningly) "So? What about her?"

Romance: (Looking sly) "I like friendship, even though some people use it as an excuse not to become involved with a potential suitor. <u>Even friends can be romantic with one another.</u>"

Me: So it doesn't affect you because Friendship was here in this world long before you were?"

Romance: "Well, I admit that gives her a definite advantage, but we are certainly a good match and we can coexist and rule intimate relationships magnificently."

Me: "Really?"

Romance: "Sure. <u>The way marriage and relationships are going these days I think genuine friendship may be the only way to fix things.</u>"

Marriage: "Well, maybe you don't have a problem with it, but I have serious concerns about the ability of people to form marital contracts and bonds on the basis of friendship principles."

Me: "Oh? Why is that?"

Marriage: (Looking at me seriously) "Because, if Friendship takes over intimate relationships as you would have it, there would be little or no need for me as I am."

Me: "But why do you think that way?"

Marriage: (Contemplative) "<u>Marriage principles and friendship principles are really not the same thing at all, even though most people want to believe otherwise.</u> When a guy gets married the rules change for him and he has to comply with them. He can't just call his sweetie any old time he wants. A good husband has to be consistently in touch and touch base with his wife daily or close to it. He needs to give reasonable explanations to his wife *for his whereabouts, associates, associations, and make promises of fidelity and monogamy. If his wife sees his friends or associates as threatening or as obstacles to the type of marriage she believes in, then she has the right to ask him to give them up. <u>If the couple based their relationship on friendship principles first and foremost the marriage expectations would change dramatically.</u>"*

Me: "How so?"

Marriage: "Because friends don't always have established expectations or rules for such things as the frequency of contacts, like phone calls, and they often don't feel a need to explain their whereabouts or associations. <u>Friends don't answer to one another as they do to a spouse,</u> so a spouse wouldn't be able to challenge her partner about his choices and decisions the way a traditional wife would. Friends usually don't mix their finances, real estate holdings, have children together, etc. So <u>when people are friends first, the marriage would be based on principles of friendship such as acceptance and genuine tolerance of differences,</u> so how could that possibly work? Marriage as we know it is more of a property and ownership type of arrangement, even if it is unconscious, and friendships generally don't operate this way."

Just then we all heard another voice speaking to us from another table. We all turned to look and hidden behind a *Los Angeles Times* newspaper we saw good old Divorce sitting nearby and listening in on our conversation.

Divorce: (With a devious grin) "She is very slow to change, Richard, so it will be difficult for her to accept friendship as the primary basis of relationships. But then, I shouldn't complain."

Me: "Hey, Divorce, I haven't seen you in decades, but I know you're doing well."

Divorce was a short, round, bald man today, but he was strong and vigorous looking. He looked healthy and happy, but he also had a slightly sinister look about him as well.

Divorce: "Yup, I'm doing just fine, thanks to these two partners in crime."

(He says with a chuckle and opens his hands and spreads them out at Romance and Marriage like a game show host.)

Marriage: "You see, Richard, he comes around because the lack of romance encourages him."

Divorce: (Smiling) "C'mon, Marriage, you know it's true. Without you I wouldn't be able to exist here, and vice versa."

Marriage: (Smiling with resignation) "Oh yeah, well I did just fine for a few eons without you."

Divorce: (Trying to annoy Marriage) "My, my, she sure has gotten testy in her old age, hasn't she?"

Romance: (Sincerely jumping to Marriage's defense) "Well, can you blame her? She really is starting to see her grip on this world slip. People are continuing to get divorced at much higher rates than ever. In fact, most marriages will end in divorce: at least sixty percent of them nowadays, as you already know, and more and more people are choosing to stay single throughout their lifetimes. Even the people who do get married are waiting until they are much older."

Divorce: (Shaking his head in mock despair) "Well, we all know that for every beginning there must be an ending. So I am just doing my job." (He bows his head sadly, but then his conniving grin reemerges.)

Marriage: (Looking at me) "Richard, did you tell this less than pleasant spirit we were meeting here?

Me: "No way, I didn't tell anyone."

Divorce: "Like you could hide from me? You might as well let me join you and put in my two cents. What could it hurt?"

Marriage: (Chuckling as if she can't believe her ears) "How about several good thirty-year marriages, that's what it could hurt."

Divorce: (Unfazed) "Well, if they were good marriages they wouldn't end because of me, now would they?"

Me: "Okay, okay, he is here now so let's let him join us."

"Make love, not war.
Hell, do both, get married!"
~ Women's restroom, The Filling Station. Bozeman, Montana ~

4

Book Four:
JUDGES OF MEN

"The supreme excellence is not to win a hundred victories in a hundred battles. The supreme excellence is to subdue the armies of your enemies without even having to fight them."
~ *Lao-Tzu* ~

Since the 1960s we have taken on a very different point of view when it comes to women's rights and liberties in the contemporary world. My mother had other T-shirts back then, besides the one I've mentioned previously, that expressed her feelings about the women's movement. "Oh Bullshit" was another of her favorites because it was so blatantly unladylike in 1960s Kansas, and it also stated clearly how she felt about being paid less than a man for doing the same job. In those days she worked for the phone company and had become the supervisor of her department, but still earned significantly less than men who had identical positions. And although she meant well, I never became particularly fond of her habit of trying to psychoanalyze me and my gender at the kitchen table over meals. I do have to admit that she was a very good listener when she had the time and I could talk to her openly about anything at all, especially about those things I knew other boys couldn't even think about within the vicinity of their moms. But in spite of her good intentions, one of the most significant things that did happen to me during that era, and to millions of other men as well, was that I became very apologetic for men and who we are. The women's movement had really heated up at this time, and I felt pummeled by the media, educational institutions, female relatives, radical feminists, and by other sources as well for the atrocities we males had been perpetrating on females throughout time.

Throughout the 1960s, 1970s, and the 1980s, women were profoundly successful in not only changing the way we act toward them and deal with them, they have also been remarkably successful in legislating their agenda and making it the law of the land. And although this has certainly been a fruitful endeavor and numerous changes have been made that were long overdue, guys have had a very difficult time adjusting in this new world. On the one hand, we guys have some very strong, natural instincts that dominate our thoughts and feelings daily, but on the other hand, we have to conform to a very rigid standard of masculinity or we are told in a variety of ways that we are a bunch of unredeemable assholes for even thinking and feeling such things.

In his book *Iron John*, Robert Bly refers to the feminist era's process of men becoming more feminine, thoughtful and gentle as "wonderful," but also "troubling" at the same time. Men became more sensitive to and considerate of others, which are good things, but they also lost touch with the inner "wild-man" that balanced them and helped to make them who they really are. The "soft male" as he calls them, became more kind and thoughtful all right, but sacrificed much of their "inner tiger" instincts and the inherent male confidence they relied upon to feel good about themselves. In turn, this sacrifice corrupted their self-identity and hampered their decision-making and self-assuredness. And nowhere is this more apparent than in our modern television shows. In the long running television series *Quantum Leap*, the main character, Dr. Sam Beckett, played by actor Scott Bakula, leaps through time from one year and situation to another. In each case, he finds himself in someone else's precarious circumstances that he must somehow repair before he is allowed to leave and leap into another time. As he tries to be the "sensitive" male, however, he politely refuses to have sex with beautiful women who offer themselves to him (yeah, right!), he lets women walk all over him in general, he lets bullies bully him, and tyrants oppress him. All the while his critical decision-making abilities are basically nonexistent because he might offend someone, God forbid, if he makes any tough choices. But by the end of each episode though, the politically correct "soft male" always manages to somehow stumble into a workable solution for every situation; he then becomes more lovable than ever. In the long-running television series *Charmed*, the story revolves around three heroine sisters who are modern-day witches and who always fight evil and strive for good. In most cases, however, any male they encounter or date, and who doesn't show the appropriate "soft male" traits, is usually identified as a demon and is inevitably vanquished from existence by the end of the show.

Not Guilty: The Case in Defense of Men is a book by David Thomas that covers the changes of the feminist era with great efficiency and positively challenges the misconceptions of maleness in the post feminist era. In contrast to the male image often promoted by modern television and Western Society in general, Thomas uses empirical data to point out the fallacies of common male convictions. I would highly recommend both this book and *Iron John* by Robert Bly to any man who wants to reconcile the confusion he still carries from this incredible time of change.

Take monogamy, for instance, which is probably the most explosive single issue that still separates the genders and causes more conflict than just about any other single issue. I can't even begin to express how many women have attacked me (verbally, of course) when I tell them I am not at a place in the relationship where I am interested in making any commitments or promises of monogamy. This is, of course, a woman's primary and most powerful negotiating tool when making The Deal, and when it is taken away they can become extremely offended and hostile. Many of my male readers would never admit this to their girlfriends or wives, and understandably so, but the vast majority of the world's male population fantasizes about a lifetime of finding new sex partners and of having multiple sex partners on a regular basis. Much to the chagrin of the politically correct, our media publications, social science publications, and movie and television productions confirm it. Anthropologists reveal that this is largely due to our evolution and that for hundreds of thousands of years males had to copulate with as many females as possible if they wanted to successfully procreate (the inner "wild-man"). And even though many of us never act on these fantasies, we have been so indoctrinated into believing we are jerks for such thoughts and feelings that we prefer to blatantly lie more often than not when our female lovers confront us about these desires. When we are busy negotiating The Deal with a new potential lover, or a current one we really wish to keep, we most often agree to their terms of serial monogamy to insure continued access to her assets. And if we don't, my goodness, the responses can often be angry, violent and hurtful.

"When a man goes on a date
he wonders if he is going to get lucky.
A woman already knows."
~ Frederick Ryder ~

I was hanging out again in Cinnamon Productions, my favorite coffee house in Seal Beach, CA, with my long time gal pal Brenda. A few years back, she married a guy named Ted who has been married twice before and has children with both previous wives. But for Brenda, Ted is her first and only spouse. Anyway, Brenda was asking me why men aren't always truthful about their feelings when the topic of monogamy came up. And here is how the conversation took form:

Brenda: "Why doesn't he just tell me the truth in the first place?"

Me: "I don't know. Do you beat him up when he does?"

Brenda: "What do you mean?"

Me: "If you ask him how he feels about something and he tells you a truth that you don't like, do you get mad at him anyway?"

Brenda: "I don't think so, but give me an example of what you mean."

Me: "Have you ever asked him about his relationships with other women?"

Brenda: "I may have."

Me: "And?"

Brenda: "I honestly don't remember his exact response, but it was pretty wishy washy, whatever it was."

Me: "What did you ask him?"

Brenda: "Well, I read in a women's magazine the men often fantasize about having sex with other women, so I asked him if this was true."

Me: "And his answer was 'wishy washy'?"

Brenda: "Yup."

Me: "Many women ask men to tell them the truth about how they feel regarding certain issues and the men know it is safer to give a politically correct answer than it is to tell the real truth."

Brenda: "Wait, how can that be?"

Me: "Well, when I tell a woman that I am not going to make promises of monogamy I often get a response that tells me she is really offended. So most of the time I just keep my mouth shut and I don't say anything at all. It's much safer that way."

Brenda: (With a major frown) "That's wrong!"

Me: "What's wrong?"

Brenda: "You can't do that. That's mistreating people."

Me: "It is?"

Brenda: (As if I should know better) "Well, yeah. You can't be with multiple women at the same time; that's abusive."

Me: "I don't think I said that, but it is?"

Brenda: "Of course it is!

Me: "Why is it always an automatic assumption that men are either monogamous or radically promiscuous? Can't there be other possibilities, options, or in betweens?"

Brenda: "Do they know about each other?"

Me: "Well, when I am seeing someone she is fully aware I have not made agreements of exclusivity, so it is a possibility I could have other women in my life. I don't go around jamming it down her throat though. And besides, just because I may be seeing other women it doesn't mean I am sleeping with them."

Brenda: (Thinking carefully) "Well, if they know…and do it anyway…"

Me: "Hey, I only date big girls who are mature and perfectly capable of making those kinds of decisions for themselves."

Brenda: But still, it just isn't right."

Me: "Why is that? Can't I enjoy the type of lifestyle I am most interested in having?"

Brenda: "No, because then you'd get what you want."

Me: "Well, that's true, and we all know men shouldn't get the things they want. What kind of immoral and disgusting world would that be?"

Brenda smiles sheepishly at me and hits me on the arm.

I am sure that men do it too, but women often ask men to be honest about their feelings, and then they beat them up verbally when the guy tells the truth and it is not the answer the women want to hear. My young cousin and his wife were visiting me from Missouri and having one of their "normal conversations" in the car, which sounded like fighting to me. She asked him a question and got a very honest, well thought-out answer that she didn't like at all, so she lit into him. Then she turned to me to look for support with her point of view. I told her it was better that I stay out of the mix, but I did point out that asking him for the truth and then beating him up when she gets it is not a good way to keep getting the truth in the future. And women usually have no idea how often they set themselves up for lies and disappointing revelations later when their men are not free to answer them honestly in the first place. I cannot begin to count the number of times I have heard women verbally beat up their lovers for giving answers they don't like. Then on other occasions when they get answers they do like they turn to me and say, "Why didn't he just tell me that in the first place?"

"How little do they see what really is,
who frame their hasty judgments upon that which seems."
~ Robert Southey ~

My young cousin and his wife recently "split the sheets," as my buddy Devon likes to say when referring to a couple who has broken up. A year or two earlier they split for a while because his wife said she would no longer have sex with him and that she was going to leave and probably divorce him. As a result, he decided to consummate a relationship at work and try to enjoy his new found freedom. When his estranged wife found out about the affair, she decided to "take him back" and said she wanted to reunite, which they did in fairly short order. When I spent this past Christmas with them I asked them both about their pending sheet splitting and she told me she was leaving my cousin because he had cheated on her and she just couldn't trust him anymore." My aunt had already pointed out to her daughter-in-law that it was she who had told her husband she wouldn't sleep with him any longer and was leaving him, so my aunt didn't see how it was "cheating" when it was the wife who had decided to break The Deal. I decided that saying it again was not a good idea and resolved to simply listen.

From my first memories to present day, we have all heard, read, and watched programs about how poorly we men have treated women over the centuries, and how it was now time for it all to change. The omnipresence of the mass media has bombarded us with information about how we men have dominated the work force, controlled the religions, controlled the governments, controlled the courts, kept women from the work force, kept women's salaries far below men's when they were allowed to work, and how we keep them from promotions. We have been blasted for starting and causing all of the wars, for beating and raping women, and for beating and raping little children. In fact, I heard so much of this when I was growing up that whenever a woman would complain to me about how poorly some man had treated her I always became the "soft male," took her side, and apologized for the guy's natural tendency to be a jerk because of his gender.

I cannot count the number of times in my own relationship history when I was really infatuated with a woman whom I eventually allowed to mistreat me, and who in return couldn't believe that I would let her get away with such abuses. But no matter how hard I tried I just couldn't bring myself to stop being the "soft male" and tell these women that their behavior was unacceptable, especially if it was from someone with whom I really wanted to continue a sexual relationship. I just knew some monster would come out of the closet and would beat the hell out of me if I offended women any further. So instead, I would often stay away and try to use my absence as a tool of protest and communication. One can imagine how well this strategy probably worked, or didn't work as was most often the case, but we all have to get our lessons. I even let a few of these women talk me into revealing some of my fondest sexual fantasies to them in private when I knew better, only to kick myself when they then backed away and acted insulted. And then I really felt stupid because they put up extra barriers after they had worked hard to literally dig the information out of me, so I learned to keep my mouth shut and say whatever it was I thought they wanted to hear.

Now don't get me wrong because I am no saint and I am certainly no victim either. I have received much worse and have dished out much worse than what I've revealed above, in more than my share of relationships, and as a result I have obtained the lessons in life that I most needed for growth and for learning. But this is *The Bible For Men*, and more than a few men have shared similar and worse experiences. The circumstances may have been very different, but the wounds were just as hurtful. And any man who is close to thirty or over will remember the feminist and post-feminist era of the male asshole: the time when we were blamed and made to pay for our forefather's behavior.

It seems unfortunate that "being a man" was lost somewhere and forsaken as machismo in its worst form. We've been told, for instance, that it is okay to be "sensitive" and that we should feel free to cry in front of women, etc. Ha! I tried that once about thirty years ago after a visiting lover had gone through my personal chest of drawers and found intimate, outdated letters from other women, and then decided to berate me and leave. I didn't cry out loud, but I did get a little "soft male" tearful because I really liked this person and didn't want her to leave; but it was one of the stupidest things I have ever done. Instead of acting guilty and apologetic, what I really needed to do was call her on the carpet for being rude and obtrusive enough to go through my private belongings and for invading my personal space and reading private letters that had absolutely nothing to do with her. And as I recall, the "soft male" response was not at all the response from me that she was really hoping to get.

> *"Difficulty, my brethren, is the nurse of greatness—a harsh nurse,*
> *who roughly rocks her foster-children into strength*
> *and athletic proportion."*
> *~ William C. Bryant ~*

We really have, in many ways, developed a society of soft apologetic men who are often deterred from being men because of the possible ridicule and consequences they may face. I personally have enjoyed the new access to thousands of women that the Internet provides us with, but it is unbelievable how often I've received hostile messages from women who want me to change my attitude and my profile and shape up to their "soft male" standards. I was talking to my friend Reckless this morning on the phone and she was relating some of her Internet experiences, and I told her about some of the hostile messages I had gotten in recent years:

Reckless*: *"Well who the hell are they to respond to your profile with a nasty message? If they don't like your profile why don't they just move on?"*

Me: "Yeah, my sentiments exactly."

Reckless: "Are you serious? They really went to all the trouble to write you and tell you that you are an asshole for the things you said about yourself in your profile?"

Me: "Yup, they really did."

Reckless: "What the hell did you say in the profile?"

Me "I just wrote that I was a very strong, confident, secure kind of guy and that I didn't tell women what they could or couldn't do, but when it comes to sex I prefer to be in charge and with the type of woman who wouldn't dream of telling her man 'no'."

Reckless: "And that pissed them off enough to send you a nasty e-mail?"

Me: "I guess so, because I got a number of e-mails that said things like 'all this site needs are guys like you to ruin it for all of us', and 'you have a serious problem; you are conceited, full of yourself' and 'you are downright scary', etc."

---

*Reckless has a real name, but I gave her *Reckless* as a nickname, and not because she really is, because she is not. Her nickname for me is "Trouble." I wonder why?

Reckless: "You're kidding. Just because you want to be in charge of sex?"

Me: "Yeah, another one sent me a long e-mail telling me that even if a woman liked the guy to be in charge that I shouldn't have said that in my profile because the only type of woman who would respond would be one who didn't care about herself and who had no self-esteem whatsoever. She really got hostile with me. Do you want to see some of these e-mails?"

Reckless: "Sure, send them right now."

Reckless and I were both sitting in front our computers at the time, so I first copied and pasted the text of my ad that the hostile women had a problem with:

"ABOUT YOU: You are easy to get along with, you take care of yourself, and you like strong, confident, independent, private, ambitious men. You are self-sufficient, independent, and you don't need a guy to tell you what to do or where to go. You are patient and willing to take your time writing to get to know me and you are not easily offended by my directness. You understand busy, ambitious men; and enjoy the return of love, kindness, warmth, and support that you give. When it comes to sex, you wouldn't dream of telling your man "no" whenever and however he wants to take you, even though you are a completely independent woman with a mind and will of your own."

Then I copied and pasted some of the hostile responses to this ad and sent the e-mail to Reckless. I was looking forward to hearing her response to them, so I waited patiently on the phone while she was reading. I could hear the surprise in her voice as she read quietly, but out loud:

"Hi, Richard, and thank you for considering me!
After reading your profound profile I feel extremely flattered.
Gee, imagine me, attracting a guy like you.
Your requirements in what are looking for are the most selfish, inconsiderate, asinine, clueless profile I have read thus far. One came awfully close from a handsome well-to-do doctor in New York, but you beat him!
Shouldn't you be advertising with the local Madam? Set up a call girl somewhere; I am most certain you will get one who is willing to be paid to put

up with the tidbits you might THROW at her. I would say toss, but you seem to be a very busy man. Not having anything that I am looking for, relationship wise. Call girls must be your forte as they do not get emotionally attached...you are looking for someone who has no need to get emotionally involved, correct? (Unless they have what? 5-10 yrs to throw away, to MAYBE earn that attachment from you?)

I don't doubt there are some idiots out there that would take your independent ass hoping they in turn MIGHT benefit from such an "arrangement," but I am not one of them.

Sorry if I have been a bit...to the point!...but your profile offends me, as I would imagine it would offend any intelligent woman not out for a buck from a guy!

I do understand with your travels and time you can't give much of nothing and that at least you were being honest in your profile; that is appreciated and I commend you for that. (Thank goodness for your arrogance and ignorance as I am sure you have no idea as to what you sound like to women) You are advertising for call girls not real women.

Not desperate!

Sincerely,

Consuela

PS: Good fucking luck! lol...and a giggle"

===

"I can't imagine any self-respecting woman actually answering your profile.

Good luck"

===

"I wouldn't dream of being with a man who demands a woman...who wouldn't dream of telling her man 'no' when he wants whatever he wants. I would tell you to go pack sand if it wasn't what I wanted to do as well.

Gosh, you sound awfully full of yourself. Who the hell died and left you in charge?

Sounds like you need one of those submissive Asian gals you read about in the back of sex magazines. Or maybe a female dog.

Good luck, pal!"

==

"It sounds by your profile you want a puppet? Someone who will jump when you say how high? Good luck in your search."

==

"Frequent flyer miles.
You're going to have to wait a long, long time, because there is not a woman of substance on this planet that is going to put up with this shit. Maybe you should try the local high school or a Russian mail order bride."

==

"I sent you the polite no thanks…but have to add this, what a creepy profile…who in their right mind adds that bit about sex and never saying no?? You must think we are nothing more than inanimate objects just put here for your pleasure…you work with 'offenders' so you must be picking up bad habits from them. I'm disgusted you even crossed my path."

==

"I just have to tell you that I'm the wrong lady for you. Good luck in finding a "whore" (that's what it sounds like you're looking for.) At least I'm glad that we got everything out in the open before we wasted each other's time.
God bless you."

==

"In forming a judgment, lay your hearts void of fore taken opinions; else, whatsoever is done or said, will be measured by a wrong rule; like them who have jaundice, to whom everything appears yellow."
~ Sir Philip Sidney ~

Reckless: "That's totally amazing.

Me: "Well, I actually got many more positive responses than negative ones, but you see how hostile women can be when they don't see or hear what they want."

Reckless: "Why do you think they are so offended by that?"

Me: "Anger is a product of fear, so I probably remind them of someone or of something unpleasant from their past."

Reckless: "Wait, I'll bet these women are so offended because they want to be in charge and they don't like the fact that you would take that power away from them."

Me: "You think?"

Reckless: "Yeah, and then those women wonder why their men go elsewhere to get what they want."

I have been saving correspondence over the years that I have received from women I have met online so I could use it as fodder for a book or an article. I know, I know; I am a sneaky devil, but I knew I'd use some of this stuff sooner or later. This probably won't give me complete absolution, but I did warn them in my profile that, "I am an aspiring writer who is always looking for good material for my work."

Here is the part of a letter I received while corresponding with an absolutely gorgeous woman who lives in South America:

"I have been thinking and wanted to share with you my thoughts...And clear also some doubts I have...So...If I am a bit rude...Take an aspirin, ok???

"First of all, I want to ask you if you really think you have time enough to start a relationship with me and one that could lead to marriage? I really like you, but you seem far and busy with many projects. I just sent you a long mail, but sat here wondering after...unless you will meet me soon enough...all these feelings will start to fade, you know that, don't you? We could anyways

be just friends. What I would also enjoy and appreciate…But I have a life going on…Daily…And dreams are never enough…You know that also…So back to earth…Is your interest in me real or just a time killer…?????"

What is it with women and all that extra punctuation? This letter really touched me because I liked this person, so I decided to be pretty informative about my plans and tell her the blunt truth. Fortunately, I am nowhere near as fragile as I once was and responses to my honesty are always welcomed, even if they are responses I don't like or don't want to hear. Nowadays I'd rather cut to the heart of the matter and move on if there doesn't seem to be any potential for a long-term gig. So here is the main text of my response to her:

"Although I believe I can love more deeply than the average man because I don't have most of the world's common concerns, I have decided that I will probably never marry again. In fact, it is this very decision that lets me love more deeply and permanently than the average man is able. Marriage in our world is too fragile and comes with too many petty jealousies, petty concerns and ways out, and there are too many requirements that I am unwilling to agree to. I would always love you and I would always come back, but I have no need to agree to traditional vows of marriage.

"I need to be able to come and go as I like, without feeling like I have to answer to anyone or explain to anyone where I've been or what I have been doing. But the traditional concepts of marriage do not allow for this type of freedom. When I think of having a lover and partner, I think of a woman who is one of my very best friends who I also happen to be involved with sexually. The more accepting a woman is the more I would want to be with her, share my life with her, take her with me on my travels, but I would always reserve the right to do as I please, whether she likes what I do or not. I would never deliberately do anything to hurt anyone because I do not believe in nor practice this type of behavior, but I love to travel the world and I have many dreams I wish to achieve. So I want the freedom to pursue these dreams without worry of offending or losing my friend and lover."

Okay, no wisecracks, I know I can be awfully wordy, but I was telling the truth and was being very open with her. So I got an immediate response and this is the first part of it:

"Dismissed! Was my first instinctive reaction. I like your intelligence, your kindness, your open mind, your ability to analyze and verbalize…But I

don't like your selfish attitude...Not willing to share all and give up...We can be friends, maybe could also be occasional lovers...But we could not be a team, a real couple."

Although I loved the *"maybe could also be occasional lovers"* part, the comments about my *"selfish attitude"* and that I am *"...Not willing to share all and give up..."* so that *"...we could not be a team, a real couple"* are the parts, of course, that I don't like. It is not because she is telling me the truth that I don't like these parts, it is because these are assumptions based on individual differences that we share. Since I am a man my attitude is "selfish," and I am "not willing to share all and give up" the necessary things that are required in making a "team," and "a real couple," so I couldn't possibly create a strong and lasting bond. I wonder what her comments would have been if I were a woman friend who shared these personal secrets with her? Then I might have been "independent, bold, daring," and possibly "courageous," wouldn't I?

"When women hold off from marrying men,
we call it independence.
When men hold off from marrying women,
we call it fear of commitment."
~ Warren Farrell ~

In all fairness to my friend, she wrote back soon after, before I had responded, and she apologized for what she considered to be rudeness on her part:

"Friends? After sending you my response I have read it maybe five or many more times...And felt I was rude with you. I need to apologize and thank you for being so truthful...Your honesty is worthy...And it makes me respect you as you are...An amazing man."

Damn! How could I not love a woman like her, even though she did become engaged to another man soon after this correspondence? I wrote back that no apologies were necessary and that it is never necessary to apologize for being who we are. And I am happy to announce that we have indeed been friends over the years and I am all the richer for knowing her. But her initial response to me is a learned response that our society has programmed into people who think we should be alike, and that men should think, act, behave and even desire like women; if we don't, we are pigs, dogs and chauvinists. And once again, there is nowhere that this has become more evident than it has become on television, especially in commercials and sitcoms. Male bashing has almost become a national pastime on the Internet and television these days and it has become a very scary and accepted part of our culture.

Take, for example, a comical version of male criticism in an e-mail that continues year after year to make the Internet joke circuit. It goes something like this:

How To Seduce A Woman:

Bring her flowers.
Remember her birthday.
Tell her she is pretty.
Give her a bubble bath.
Buy her chocolates.
Send her cards.
Buy her perfume.
Call her daily.
Tell her you love her.
Give her a massage.
Treat her to a facial.
Give her romantic dinners.
Light the candles.
Take her away for a romantic weekend.
Take her abroad.

How To Seduce A Man:

Show up naked with a six pack.

Another common and accepted example of male bashing on the Internet is illustrated by the following poem titled "Moods" and is an e-mail that has been circulated a few million times as well:

The Moods of a Woman:

An angel of truth and a dream of fiction,
A woman is a bundle of contradiction,
She's afraid of a wasp, will scream at a mouse,
But will tackle a stranger alone in the house.
Sour as vinegar, sweet as a rose,
She'll kiss you one minute, then turn up her nose,
She'll win you in rage, enchant you in silk,
She'll be stronger than brandy, milder than milk,
At times she'll be vengeful, merry and sad,
She'll hate you like poison, and love you like mad.

The Moods of a Man:

Hungry.
Horny.
Sleepy.

Here is a facsimile diagram of a man's brain that a relative sent to me and that has been going around the Internet circuit as well. As anyone can see, all of the crude criticisms and primitive labels men receive are illustrated by this drawing:

THE MALE BRAIN

"There is only one corner of the universe
you can be certain of improving
and that's your own self."
~ Aldous Huxley ~

Although I can certainly see the humor in these jokes and cartoons and can readily admit to major differences of the genders, similar e-mails abound by the thousands, and the majority of them are much less nice to men than the softer examples I have chosen. And how about the endless television commercials such as the one where the man only wants the Sport Utility Vehicle because it is a hotrod, but the wife wants it because it is practical and safe for their child? Or, how about the beer commercial where the guys are talking like idiots about naked women wrestling in mud while their dates just sit there and shake their heads in disgust? Another favorite is the cell phone commercial where the father gives his two teenaged daughters new cell phones, but they act offended when he implies he has given them the phones to stay in touch with him. When the mother says they can call their friends who have the same service for free the girls jump to embrace her, but completely ignore the father. As the good "soft male" he is, the father just stands there like a whipped puppy and pleads "call me" once again as the girls walk away. And what about the endless sitcoms we've been subjected to in which the men are often depicted as the fumbling fools without a lick of good sense and the women as the stable, intelligent, pragmatic, guru-glue that holds the world together and who constantly fixes all of the carnage that the male fools have created? Of course, this goes on episode after episode without the men ever really learning their lessons. The networks are jammed with these commercials and sitcoms every night of the week.

I love Tim Allen and he is one of the funniest and best actors I have ever seen, but *Tool Time* was not a show that favored or promoted the intelligence and wisdom of men. I suppose it started with the humor behind Archie Bunker and *All In The Family*, because this show was conceived and aired during the early stages of the feminist era, which also initiated the era of the male asshole: when men were first becoming apologetic for who we are and for the chauvinist actions of our forefathers. Even the spin off sitcom *The Jefferson's* depicted a successful businessman and father whose wife constantly had to apologize for his bigotry, bad taste, the messes he created with his neighbors, and his insensitive humor.

Long gone are the days of television shows like *Father Knows Best* and *My Three Sons,* which were programs that depicted men as wise, caring, responsible leaders of their families and communities. Instead, we have replaced these more positive role models with characters like Al Bundy from *Married With Children,* Homer Simpson from *The Simpsons,* and Hank from *King Of The Hill.* And what an incredible change in society's perception of maleness this demonstrates.

"Right is right, even if everyone is against it;
and wrong is wrong, even if everyone is for it."
~ William Penn ~

****

Marriage: (Sincerely) "Richard, women are going to agree with your e-mail friend that you are being selfish and even greedy for not agreeing to marry or to at least make promises of monogamy in exchange for her participation in a relationship with you."

Divorce: (Smiling) "It's the stuff that conflicts are made of."

Me: "Yeah, I thought about that too. But this is a book for men, so I'll just have to take the heat. Besides, I don't need to have sex with her to be her friend."

Marriage: "Many women are also going to think you are acting like a victim and are only pointing out the negative side of relationships to try and portray men as being victims who have been castrated by women."

Me: "I suppose that is possible because it is certainly easier than admitting any complicity to gender conflict, but my stories are really just my way of relating to men who feel misunderstood and disenfranchised by social misconceptions and flawed relationships. There is no one to blame, but I think someone has to give men permission to be who they are and to feel the way they really feel."

Divorce: "I doubt many women will even read your book."

Romance: "I agree with Richard. Men need to learn to be a lot more honest with women, even if women don't like what they have to say."

Me: "Exactly. <u>This political correctness nonsense is getting out of hand and men have to quit participating in it</u>. <u>We only say what we think</u> women want to hear, all too often."

Divorce: "Oh, I don't know. I think it has its advantages."

Marriage: "Well, <u>it seems logical that men are much more likely to find the kind of relationships they want if they would be more honest about their feelings and what they want</u>. But if men become completely honest about their feelings and desires it is likely the marriage rate will drop dramatically as a result."

Me: "Yeah, it is amazing how many men don't tell women the truth because they know they're not going to like it. But then again, some men can be rather militant too, so they have to learn to get over their hurts and grudges and move on."

Romance: "I guess this is the place where friendship is supposed to take over and help out."

Me: "Well it certainly couldn't hurt."

"Even if you're on the right track,
you'll get run over if you just sit there."
~ Will Rogers ~

5
Book Five:
THE 1st CHRONICLES
OF SERIAL MONOGAMY

"Confusing monogamy with morality has done more
to destroy the conscience of the human race
than any other error."
~ George Bernard Shaw ~

It wasn't God who outlawed polygamy; it was the kings, religious rulers and the governments who ended it in most parts of the world, and not because it was morally reprehensible and therefore sinful and wrong. It was outlawed by the kings and rulers of the time because men had too many wives and children without the financial means to support them, and the evolving urban sprawl had become awash in poverty and squalor, which eventually lead to disease, crime, costly law enforcement and prison construction. So the real downfall of it was the practical and necessary economic relief that reason demanded. And back then there were powerful spiritual rulers, like the Holy Roman Emperor or Pope, who also wielded considerable political power and decided to make affordable families a spiritual issue to aid in the enforcement of changing laws. Even in America the U.S. government forced Utah to outlaw the practice of polygamy before they would approve the territory's application for statehood, but this was primarily for the purpose of imposing their moral beliefs upon the territory, which was the very thing they didn't want England or France to do to them. And nowadays, our society in general touts serial monogamy as if it were the holy grail of our spiritual time and development.

In the movie *Colors*, an older and more experienced policeman, played by Robert Duval, is giving some advice to a young rookie who is not very receptive, played by Sean Penn. To get the young officer to drop his defenses and listen to an older cop he decides to tell a story so the rookie can infer his primary point. It appears the young cop has some rather rigid opinions about life and the older cop wants him to open himself to other options and possibilities. So he tells him about a young bull that goes running to the top of a hill where papa bull is observing the herd of cows below. As the youngster approaches his father he yells, "Hey, Dad, let's run down this hill and catch a cow so we can fuck her." But the older and wiser bull just gives the youngster a puzzled look then calmly replies, "Why would I want to do that, when I can walk down this hill and fuck them all?"

Although the majority of men will see the humor and inherent male nature of this story and will likely find that it has some poignant implications, the majority of women are most likely going to find it offensive because of our obvious gender differences. But the most significant meaning for men and women alike should be the implied understanding and realization that serial monogamy is the instinctual product of the matriarchal consciousness and not the product of men's. Yet we men have promoted, peddled, plugged, hyped and reinforced this practice as if we really believed in it, only to turn around and hold our sons and daughters to completely different standards and expectations of sexual conduct. Young men are supposed to sow their wild oats and enjoy their youth, but young women are supposed to remain virtuous, uncorrupted and untouched. So who the hell are the guys supposed to be having sex with?

As the 1960s and 1970s unfolded and women were winning liberation in all social dimensions, another aspect of The Deal began to take shape. Although women were enjoying their newly won freedoms to have sexual relationships with whomever they chose and whenever they chose, the stigma of promiscuity followed them and so did unpleasant labels such as "whore," "loose," and "slut." Instinctually, socially and emotionally, women struggled to reconcile this social contradiction and they did so mainly by reverting to their age old instinctual practice of serial monogamy. According to anthropologist Dr. Helen Fisher in her book *The Anatomy Of Love*, it was the practice of women for a period of roughly three hundred thousand years to couple exclusively with a male for an average of about four years to give birth, rear the offspring to an age where he or she could react defensively when in danger, then find a new mate and do it again. So the evolution of this "four-year itch" and switch technique for women to pick one man at a time, then move on later, is what gives them comfort and justification for their current standard and method of sexual promiscuity. If it feels good instinctually then it will also feel more natural and much better morally, and this is largely the contribution that has created the current custom and conventional wisdom we've come to know as serial monogamy. Men wanted women to have sex with them without having to marry them, so women took the opportunity for this sexual liberation by making men promise to be exclusive, just like them, to help avoid the appearance and stigma of being a loose woman.

> *"Monogamy is the Western custom of one wife*
> *and hardly any mistresses."*
> *~ H.H. Munro (Saki) ~*

I think it is a damn shame that many men still try to use the weapon of dishonor and humiliation against women when women choose to be with someone other than them because this behavior only serves to exacerbate the larger problem of gender conflict in general. And it keeps both genders trapped in a hypocritical cycle of conflicting social standards through the adult practice of teaching one thing to maturing boys and girls and then modeling another. But there is also another major issue besides this type of hypocrisy, although more subtle, that has grown from the social practice of trading exclusivity for sexual access.

In countless studies and surveys of women's sexual practices that have been conducted by social scientists and numerous women's magazines alike, we have identified many things that turn women on and many things that turn women off. Many women, for example, love to receive oral sex and give it; many enjoy long periods of foreplay, wearing sexy lingerie, being held down, having their nipples pinched or bitten, doing a striptease, etc. But the number one turnoff for nearly all women across the board is a man who likes to indulge in cross-gender behaviors, such as cross-dressing and role playing where *he* takes the role of *she*. So in other words, when we try to be more like women, they become less interested in us.

Isn't it interesting that we've pursued a policy and social trend in the Western world of getting men to be more like women when this is actually the very behavior that makes us less attractive to them? Being androgynous doesn't mean we have to give up the things that make us male; it means that we learn to accept the parts of ourselves that we have in common with females. But when we negotiate away those very attributes and instincts that do make us men, especially to get laid, the result is a confusing set of hypocritical standards to live by and the consequence of becoming less appealing to the very gender we are most concerned with seducing.

In general, men are considered morally corrupt when we act on our instincts to have multiple partners, so we are constantly pressured to be more like women. But when we do become more like women we are less attractive to them and we are then bewildered by the endless, consistent, nagging drive to go out and "score." So we are damned if we do and we are damned if we don't, and then women are confused and constantly wonder why men "cheat."

But to probe serial monogamy deeper, we need to go back to where we left the coffee house interviews, because other guests are about to join our group. If Divorce knew about our gathering, one can bet that others had gotten wind of it as well. Although the awareness of these spirits or "Inorganic Beings" is slow, it acts superbly once it has decided on a course of action:

Me: "So Divorce, you must consider yourself completely dependent upon Marriage for your survival?"

Divorce: "Indeed, this is so, because as I have said, without the beginning there can be no ending. But then again, these are just words because I am also a beginning as well."

Me: "Yes, you are a beginning of a new single life, aren't you?"

Marriage: "Like there is a need for an end to me?"

Me: "Well, how could there be a beginning to something that had no ending?"

Romance: "Yeah, nothing like a little war to make people appreciate and enjoy peace, huh?"

Marriage: "Traditionally, physical death has been the only appropriate ending to a couple's union. But as much as I hate to admit it, there are many couples who fight and who are so hateful to each other that they really do need to stop the conflict and go their own way."

Me: "It never ceases to amaze me how people can be so intimate with one another by sharing their body fluids night after night and all aspects of their lives, only to turn and end their love affair in a nasty, hostile, and vicious war."

Divorce: (Looking a little defensive) "Hey, don't blame me for the way people act when they split the sheets. I don't require all of the fighting, bickering, and hateful behavior that goes on up to and during the end of a marriage. I have nothing to do with that nonsense and it is totally unnecessary (he stops to ponder for just a moment then continues with), although it certainly helps to seal the finality of The Deal."

Marriage: "Well, even if you are not solely to blame, those two you hang out with certainly promote your cause. Between the three of you there is so much havoc that there is no wonder marriage is failing."

Me: (Looking at Divorce) "What two that you hang out with?"

Just then another voice enters through the front door and we hear a boisterous

"Us!"

We all turn to look and in walks Jealousy with Serial Monogamy closely following behind. Jealousy looks disheveled as usual, like she just got out of bed after sleeping in her clothing. Her poorly-fitted, light-colored sack dress is crumpled high on large heavy breasts so that it doesn't hang to her knees in the front like it should. And her long brunette hair is hanging down, uncombed, with a big lump on the top rear of her head as if her pillow had permanently mashed it forward. Serial Monogamy looks like a thirty-something yuppie wife from the suburbs with manicured nails, nicely-styled hair, expensive jewelry, tight fitting clothes, pumps, and an absolutely luscious body. Sometimes she looks really soft and warm, then other times she has a rather hard looking edge about her.

Monogamy: (Smilingly at me) "Hey, lover, long time no see. (She turns and looks at Marriage) I disagree that marriage is failing."

Marriage: "Oh? How many times have you been married and divorced?"

Monogamy: "Several, as you well know."

Divorce: "And you call that working?"

Monogamy: "Well, yeah."

Me: "Hi, ladies, I guess you two came with Divorce?"

Monogamy: "Yes, indeed, we go most places with him and Marriage. (Smiling deviously) They don't know how to act without us."

Romance: "They are always hanging around me too. Any time they think The Deal is going to be negotiated they appear."

Jealousy: (Looking at Romance) "Well, you're not much good in those types of situations, so we have to be there to make sure a proper agreement is reached."

I get out of my seat and push a couple of tables together and then I give the ladies their chairs.

Me: "Have a seat, girls; we made plenty of room for you."

Monogamy: (Talking while taking her seat) "Yes, and The Deal has to be an agreement that serves our purposes. If we left that up to him (pointing at Romance) there would be no agreements and people would just get into bed and start screwing each other's brains out."

Jealousy: *"Some type of repercussions for punishment have to be established early on, or the world would just fuck and fuck until everyone became bored with it, or (looking at me) you'd all get some disease and would wipe out your own species."*

Me: *"Wow, that's some serious self-image you have going on there."*

**"Heaven has no rage like love to hatred turned,
Nor hell a fury like a woman scorned."**
~ William Congreve ~

Jealousy: *"Okay, maybe you humans have grown a tiny bit beyond your primal instincts, but you are all still a bunch of idiots, especially you men."*

Me: *"What? You believe that men still think exclusively with their penises?"*

Monogamy: *(Looking self-righteous) "Well, isn't that why you guys give your dicks names? Because they think for you and give you orders? We all know how much you hate to take orders from total strangers."*

The whole group breaks out with hysterical belly laughter and they bang on the tables and stomp their feet. It takes them a while to finally calm back down, but they eventually do. There is only one other customer in the coffee house at the time who is an older lady, and she only looks blankly at us from across the room as she sips her java. The early morning customers are used to my buddies and I who include the owner of the coffee house and other local businessmen that gather there to talk about politics, women and business. That group can get pretty boisterous as well, and a few of them laugh louder than my comfort zone often allows, so this group isn't unusual and doesn't attract much attention.

Divorce: *"Men don't respond well to ultimatums either."*

Monogamy: *"So? We still love to give them anyway. Besides, men have double standards because they want to have multiple partners, but threaten us with abandonment if we fool around on them."*

Me: "Hormones are a powerful influence on younger men for sure. But after a certain age it is not enough just to have a naked body next to us because our hormones no longer rule. Usually, by the time a guy is in his thirties or forties he is thinking differently."

Jealousy: "But he can still be manipulated by the right partner through the possibility of sex."

Me: (Just a little defensive, but not much) "So you and Monogamy really believe the fate of the human race lies with you?"

Monogamy: "Well, think about it. Without us, who would contain rampant sexual activity, and therefore control the planet's birth and disease rate?"

Me: "Hey, monogamous marriages or not, the planet's population is growing at astronomical rates. And I happen to know that AIDS is spreading like wildfire in third world countries where serial monogamy is widely practiced. Besides, common sense is still pretty available these days."

Jealousy: "Ha! Common Sense! That old coot. I can kick her ass just by making her think that someone is going to get laid without her permission or knowledge. (She motions toward Divorce with a nod of her head) That's how I cause so many to give into Divorce here, you know?"

Monogamy: (Smiling deviously) "That's right, follow the rules and guidelines I have set forth or Jealousy here will take you to a dark place and we'll devour you whole."

That's what I like about the "Inorganic Beings"—they pretty much tell it like it is and are not much for pulling punches. If someone really wants to know the truth, just ask an Inorganic Being and expect a pretty direct answer. But it is wise not to ask if the answer is not welcomed, because they will certainly respond unabashedly.

Me: (Looking at Jealousy) "I'm pretty much over you these days, but I do remember when I used to summon you a lot. Back then I thought you were me and that I had no choice but to let you take over my entire being."

Jealousy: "*Yeah, isn't it great? Most people don't realize that as youngsters they learned to turn themselves over to me, just like they learned to train their bladder and bowels to wait until they were sitting on the toilet. It was as much work for them to learn to give into me as it would be for them to learn to give me up. And since <u>older peoples' points of view become more rigid with age, it's not likely they'll be interested in learning a new response,</u> so I don't have much to worry about.*"

Monogamy: "*A good dose of jealousy is important to any love relationship, so people don't forget about their agreements to honor and worship me above any other agreement. And when they cheat, all I have to do is sic <u>Jealousy</u> on them, and she <u>brings Revenge, Betrayal and Self-Importance with her.</u> Now those are some mean bitches who can kick some royal human butt.*"

Me: "*I find it extremely difficult to accept that anyone would really think Jealousy is good for a relationship, let alone Revenge, Betrayal and Self-Importance.*"

Monogamy: "*Oh, did I say they were good for a relationship? Well, what I meant to say is that they are good for me, and I usually rule the relationship. So what is good for me IS good for the relationship. No?*"

Romance: "*Sure, if you think panic, high blood pressure, spousal abuse, beatings and murder are good for relationships too.*"

Divorce: "*Hey, the combination of monogamy and jealousy create the biggest share of my customers, so I can't complain. Without them there would be no infidelity and little or no betrayal, so fewer customers for me.*"

Monogamy: "*Well what's the point of being married if there is no monogamy?*"

Romance: *(He points to me with a nod of his head)* "*Well, if Richard has his way, Friendship will dominate the future of love affairs and the majority of you could be out of jobs (he starts to laugh at his own humor.) <u>Friendship</u> has been kicking your asses for an eternity now because she <u>has so much more staying power,</u> so you can kiss your food bye-bye from this world when people eventually catch on.*" *(He chuckles again at his own words.)*

Jealously: (Rolling her eyes) "That's not very likely."

Marriage: "I would have to agree with her."

Monogamy: (Looking a bit smug) "Not any time real soon anyway. Besides, who wants to sleep with their friends? That sounds really weird to me."

Jealousy: "Yeah, the rules and conditions for a physically intimate relationship have to change. You have to hold your lover to a much different and higher set of standards than what you expect of your friends, don't you see?"

Me: "Yes, I see that as a great condition for you to feed on."

Monogamy: "People have been reared and conditioned to dream of spouses and lovers as different from all others and to see and hold them as special and unique. So it isn't likely they will just step out of the conceptual box they are most familiar with to fully examine such a foreign notion."

Me: "I can't imagine picking a family member, such as a sister, brother, grandmother, aunt, or my father or mother to live with the rest of my life and to mix all of my finances and all other life aspects with. And yet, this is exactly what we do; only we call them a wife or husband."

Jealousy: "Most people do not think independently enough from us to really look outside the normal parameters of behavior, Richard, let alone explore them, and you know this, so why waste your time?"

Me: "Don't be too sure of yourselves. As you know, I am writing a book titled The Bible For Men *and I expect it to be a worldwide best-selling success and to eventually be published in many languages, so it could reach millions, if not billions of people in the future, even after I'm gone. Besides, I know that aspects of each of you already exist in other worlds where these concepts are fully developed and practiced."*

Jealousy: (Looking around the room) "Did Arrogance show up when I wasn't looking? Hell, see what happens when you leave the fuckin' door open? Anyone can just walk right in."

They all look at me for a brief moment, then burst out laughing again. Jealousy bobs her head with a big smile as if she is proud of herself and her quick wit.

Monogamy: *"Come on, Richard, you really don't believe you can change billions of people's minds about us, do you? Just be happy with what we give you. You get to have numerous relationships and love affairs if you want them; you just have to do them one at a time. So what's the big deal? If you don't like one woman, get rid of her and find another."*

Me: *"The big deal is the dumping part. That is a big time set up for Jealousy, Betrayal, and Nasty Break Ups to wreak havoc with our lives, not to mention some unpleasant karma down the road."*

Jealousy: *"Yeah, Richard, have a sense of humor and relax. Give up this book thing because you know that we have a purpose here too."*

Me: *"I never implied otherwise, but I know that solid, long-term love affairs are more pleasant, better off in general, and more likely to occur without you in the midst of them."*

Monogamy: *"You men just need to get over yourselves and stop using your instinctual traits as an excuse. You don't have to let your instincts rule you."*

"I am into parallel monogamy."
~ Anonymous ~

Me: *"That's real easy for you to say. Serial monogamy is a much more natural state of being for women."*

Monogamy: *"Yeah, it is, so get over it."*

Me: *"That would be similar to telling women to get over their instincts to give birth and become mothers. If a woman gets married or becomes part of a couple and agrees not to have children then later changes her mind, it's okay for her and she is often applauded for her decision and the courage to recant. But if a man agrees to a monogamous marriage or relationship and later changes his mind, he is an asshole, a jerk, or a dog."*

Jealousy: "And you don't think women like variety and change their minds about being monogamous with some guys?"

Me: "Sure they do, and a huge number of them end up fooling around, but they almost always replace their boredom by creating another serial monogamous relationship."

Monogamy: "You know, Richard, I think you still have issues. I think you are just trying to discredit and destroy the belief in love, commitment and serial monogamy in the eyes of men."

Jealousy: "Yeah, it sounds like you are depicting yourself and men in a role of male subservience, and trying to move to a position of power. What you are missing here is the love."

Monogamy: "This is a sad way to look at relationships, a kind of one-sided view on marriage and commitment. What fears you must have. I can't help but wonder how many dysfunctional relationships cause a man like you to feel this way."

Me: "So anyone who stands in contrast to the normal way things are done is a mental moron with issues?"

Monogamy: "Yes, but look at it this way. Women like to have multiple partners too, but they are simply more content to do them one at a time. It makes them feel moral and righteous, and what's wrong with that?"

Divorce: "Don't you just love how women can always justify their behavior?"

Me: "What's wrong with this is the moral high ground that is taken. You believe a woman is morally superior when she has six lovers because she does them one at a time. If a guy has six lovers he is an asshole if he has more than one at a time. But the end result is the same; they both have multiple lovers."

Monogamy: (Smiling coyly) "Yeah, so what?"

Me: "Come on, don't act so innocent with me, you know exactly how this is often used."

Romance: (Smiling broadly) "Yeah, the number of women who cheat has grown over the years to either match or even exceed the number of men who do. But I know what Richard is talking about; he is talking about the women who use serial monogamy like a weapon or power tool and make the guy promise to give up his other women if he wants to be with them, then they dump the guy as soon as he doesn't measure up. (Eyeing me in mock suspicion) I don't suppose that has ever happened to you, Richard?"

Everyone looks at me again and erupts into loud laughter. I act just a little chagrined to humor them and then laugh along with the group.

Me: "I'll admit that I know a large number of men who have experienced this little maneuver and it's made some of them a little bitter, that's for sure. But I have to admit that I am a bit tired of modern women acting like they are morally superior to men because society has treated serial monogamy as a deity for so long. I know that men have largely brought it upon themselves in their effort to control women's sexual behavior throughout the millennia, but I am pretty sure there are lots of men out there who are rethinking this part of The Deal."

Monogamy: (Dismissively) "Oh? And what gives you that impression?"

Romance: "The number of people who are choosing to stay single and become single is a loud and blatant signal."

Marriage: "And people are waiting much longer to marry these days too."

Me: "Well, the most obvious of the signs is probably prenups. Although they are just the beginning, prenuptial agreements are the first stage of contract marriage. And these contracts already incorporate expiration dates along with their performance clauses. So eventually they are very likely to add expiration dates to the entire marriage contract itself."

Marriage: (Perks up when she hears this comment) "What kind of performance clauses are you talking about?"

Me: "The ones that determine settlements if divorce or infidelity occurs before and after certain time frames."

Marriage: (Becoming very interested) "And what expiration dates?"

Divorce: "I know what he is talking about, and I don't think they are a long way off either, maybe several years down the road at most, but it is likely to come very soon."

Romance: "He's talking about time limited marriage contracts that come up for renewal or that expire once the children are twenty-one years of age and out of college, or anytime after they turn eighteen and go out on their own.

Marriage: "I knew people were becoming very creative with marriage agreements, but I can't imagine that too many will actually allow the entire marriage to expire. So what about renewal clauses?"

Divorce: "Yeah, some people are disregarding the normal marriage ceremony and marriage license and are creating their own arrangements entirely."

Romance: "And that's not all."

Marriage: (Shaking her head in wonder) "Wow, this has become such a widespread epidemic already. I've heard about the contracts and have witnessed numerous versions of them, but I am astonished by the level of sophistication they are reaching."

Divorce: "Yeah, it seems primarily to be a practice of wealthy and upper-middle class people, and gay couples too, who don't want to lose their money and homes to ex-spouses, but who still like the idea of having a family environment."

Romance: "The guys like it because there is an equal split of responsibility for child support and custody. And no alimony is involved either, unless of course it is built into the contract, or the guy continues to receive sexual privileges for continued economic support that goes beyond the boundaries of the agreement."

Monogamy: "So if the marriage is going well the contract can be renewed?"

Romance: "Sure, why not?"

Me: "People are living so much longer than ever that this causes new levels of difficulty and our age spans are still increasing dramatically. Within a few decades people will live so long that marriages will have to last over incredible lengths of time:"

Romance: "And no matter how romantic this sounds the practice of being married for 70, 80, and 90 or more years may be far from practical, the way it is practiced now anyway."

"The important thing is not to stop questioning."
~ Albert Einstein ~

6

Book Six:
PROVERBS OF THE
SOCIAL MIND

*"The whole drift of my education goes to persuade me
that the world of our present consciousness
is only one out of many worlds of consciousness that exist."
~ William James ~*

We are born with one mind, but we grow up with two. The body's mind, the one we are born with, is full of instinct, a natural curiosity for life, and a keen sense of knowing what is what. This mind is the one that is operating when the telephone rings and we instantly know, without any reason, who is calling before we pick up the receiver to say "hello." It tells us of a loved one who has been hurt in an accident before we have been notified and it warns us about danger when there is no discernable reason for caution. It tells us when a lover is cheating on us even when there is no tangible evidence to prove or even suspect that such a thing is occurring, and it signals us that pending actions may not turn out as we like. The body's mind is a sudden feeling of knowing without any tangible reason we can latch on to. And then there is the social mind, the second mind that is a foreign installation and has been placed in us with help of the Inorganic Beings, our families, and society as a whole.

The social mind is the mind that was installed after birth by the powerful, omnipresent adult force that is constantly hovering around us as we grow and form our thoughts, ideas and beliefs about the world. This mind is set up by direct training, subterfuge, coercion, and sometimes through brutal physical force. It is software that reacts to certain stimuli and input the way a computer reacts to pushing the F1 or shift buttons. It tells us that we should act or react this way and that way; that we should treat adults a certain way; that we should ignore the night visions known as dreams; that we should be in church on Sundays; that we shouldn't eat meat on Fridays; that we should stop to pray at a certain time each day; that we should wait until marriage to have sex; that we shouldn't question the authority of the church or the government; that patriotism and loyalty are automatically deserved by those in authority who are giving the orders; and that fairytales about Prince Charming are to be taken literally. In fact, the social mind is set up with such tremendous force and permanence that it actually takes over for the body's mind and suppresses it to the point where we can no longer detect it for the majority of our lives. If the social mind says that eating yogurt on Sundays is a sin, then it becomes an axiom in our lives, and the guilt that follows when we slip up is our god telling us he is going to punish us for our heresy.

The vast majority of the human race makes its daily and moment by moment decisions with the social mind and not the body's mind. Because we have been doing this from a very young age that we can no longer recall, we tend to believe that the social mind is our own concoction of beliefs and convictions. But it is not difficult to understand that we believe in things without any memory, history, or personal experience of events that brought us to certain conclusions on our own. We know that if we had been born in another society that our beliefs, convictions and lives would be totally different, but rarely do we question the automatic responses of jealousy, anger, pettiness, envy, possessiveness, hurt, righteousness, and pain that certain stimuli evoke in us. Even when something deep inside is telling us that our response to stimuli is not appropriate, the social mind takes over and convinces us of our right to be offended, and of our right to exact some type of revenge.

As a student of psychology and a fledgling marriage counselor, I learned quickly that it is not divorce by itself that damages relationships and children so badly. It is rather the conviction of the social mind that tells us we should feel betrayed, assaulted, battered and terribly offended by the actions or inactions of a spouse we have just convicted and found guilty. And it is this voice that creates within us the state of being that leads us to a vicious war with someone who was supposed to be our lover, our best friend, and partner throughout life. It fascinates me that we can love someone so much that we can devote our entire lives to them, only to turn around to war with them after a few months or years.

When I was in Texas, my buddy Jackson left one summer for a little vacation to go home and attend a high school reunion. When he returned he announced that he had reestablished an old romance he had during his high school years. It was clear he was really smitten with this woman when he told me she was coming down to visit and that "she may be the one." And within a few short months he moved back to Oregon and set up house with her.

I talked to him after they set up house and even stopped by to visit a year or so later. In fact, he appeared to be a very content and happy man, so I figured this relationship was going to last for the long haul. I know when I see a buddy in love and I had never heard him speak so highly about a woman the way he spoke of this one. I corresponded with him over the next few years, but eventually we lost contact after this because our lives were on totally different paths. He had gotten married and was starting a family while I moved to California, lived by the beach, and thoroughly enjoyed the single guy lifestyle.

After several years had passed, Jackson called me up out of the clear blue to say hello. I was very curious about his married life and his wife so within a few moments I asked about her by name and how she was doing.

"That bitch!" he responded offensively upon hearing her name. "We're divorced now."

> *"And what's romance?*
> *Usually, a nice little tale*
> *where you have everything as you like it,*
> *where rain never wets your jacket*
> *and gnats never bite your nose*
> *and it's always daisy-time."*
> *~ D. H. Lawrence ~*

When something new comes along we are all too often reluctant to consider its merits if it doesn't fit with the preconceptions, perceptions, and general guidelines that our social mind was programmed to accept. It took ten thousand years before we finally accepted an alternative to *arranged marriage* and let romantic unions take prominence. And in many societies and subcultures within the Western world *arranged marriage* still has not given way to romantic unions and may not for many more years to come. Even when it is a practical, forward-moving change for the society at large, the motivation to accept the change is minimal at best and the possibility of change is relatively small.

The social mind is the part of us that buys into religious dogma and makes us go to war in the name of God. It convinces us that our crusades for fairness and righteousness are justified and that there is no other way to salvation except for the path we believe in and preach. Although many philosophers, historians, and writers can easily point out the commonalities of numerous religions and spiritual belief systems, our social minds tell us not to listen or to even consider the possibility that we share a common God and convictions. So we continue in our conflicts with one another because we believe our way to be the best, most just, and sole pathway to salvation.

"There is only one religion, though there are a hundred versions of it."
~ George Bernard Shaw ~

It is no different with relationships and the way we have developed into creating them since giving up the ancient practice of arrangement. Most people cannot think of creating a relationship with someone unless they first feel the infatuation, chemistry and passion that we so often associate with love and desire. But it rarely if ever occurs to anyone that this chemistry and passion can be built through friendships, because this is not a product of the social mindset of our cultures that practice romantic unions. Numerous people in arranged marriages, however, report that they eventually became passionate lovers once they had established the basis and foundation for a strong and enduring friendship.

Until we are willing to accept the remote possibility that there are other methods of building enduring intimacy with lovers than what we are most familiar with, there is little chance for growth. And the culprit who keeps us from believing in other possibilities is usually that foreign installation we now know as the social mind.

"If we would build on a sure foundation in friendship, we must love our friends for their sakes rather than for our own."
~ Charlotte Bronte ~

****

Back to where we left off at the coffee house discussion:

Marriage: *"Would someone explain to me how prenuptials or a contract marriage is going to improve the marital lives of people in general?"*

Jealousy: (In a huffy voice) "I don't know either. In fact, I'm not sure I like it one bit."

Monogamy: "Hey, keep in mind that prenuptial agreement clauses are voided by the courts on many occasions, especially when infidelity is involved and not covered in the contract."

Divorce: "I don't think I like this contract marriage idea either. There is very little need for divorce if it isn't a union that is sealed by the normal marriage license."

Romance: "I don't see what the debate is about, because prenuptials are here to stay and they are only going to get more detailed and specific."

Me: "I don't know, Marriage, I think this contract marriage thing may be a reprieve for you in the long run."

Marriage: (Appears to be genuinely interested) "Oh? How do you come to this conclusion?"

Romance: "I know. Because it is still a form of marriage, so it gives you new life, even if it is not a permanent arrangement at first."

Me: "Yeah, it could even serve to revitalize you and give you more youthful energy and a new, more youthful appearance. But the more important issues are that married people would have to stop treating each other as property and would have to give more respect to individual choice and differences. They would have to become more accepting and flexible like friends, or risk the possibility of the contract being voided."

Suddenly, a new voice chimes in as another uninvited guest enters the coffee house and stands looking over us. *"I am not sure I like it either."*

Jealousy: (With a big smile on her face) "Hey, Self-Importance! Welcome to the circle of fools, babe."

Self-Importance: "Hi, you bunch of hooligans. Were you trying to gang up on ol' Richard here without me?"

Self-Importance had always appeared to me as a gorgeous, seductive temptress who dressed to kill, with lean shapely legs, a firm tight butt, and large full breasts. Sometimes she was Caucasian, other times she was Hispanic, Asian, Middle Eastern, and even African. She had owned me for years and had dictated the vast majority of my love affairs and relationships in general. Even to this day I had to constantly be on guard with her because she knew all of my weaknesses and all of my buttons. On occasion, she would even enter my dreams where she would talk to me in my sleep and even seduce me there when she could. And, of course, she always had to have a complaint about something.

Me: "Well, I am not surprised to see you."

Romance: (With a devious grin) "Hey, baby, I hear that you and ol' Richard here used to be an item?"

Self-Importance: "What can I say? The boy used to have really good taste. (She looks around the coffee house) Now he takes his guests to dives like coffee houses. (She shakes her head and looks at me) I thought I taught you better, Richey, honey."

Me: (Clearing my throat) Ahem...Yeah, well...moving right along."

Self-Importance: "What's the matter, honey; don't you want anyone to know about us?"

Me: "Like they don't already know everything?"

Self-Importance: (Teasingly) "Well, what about these millions of readers who are going to buy your book and read it?" (She stands there staring at me and waits for me to get up and pull her chair out for her.)

Me: "I think all of them already have their own relationship with you and know you intimately themselves." (I decide to humor her and offer her the chair.)

Self-Importance: "Oh, Richard, darling, you can be such a bore."

Me: "And that's why you are always after me?"

Self-Importance: "Hmmm...don't flatter yourself, honey; you are food just like the rest of the human cattle. The only difference is that you know about me and are wise to a few of my seductions."

Self-Importance turned the chair I'd given her around and pulled it up close to me. She hiked her already short skirt a little, spread her beautiful legs and sat in the chair backwards so the back of the chair was separating her legs and I could see up to her crotch. The rest of them watched her antics and then laughed at me.

Romance: "Yup, same ol' Richard. He always was a sucker for a great set of legs, a nice ass, and big knockers."

The rest of them just watched the show and laughed out loud as Self-Importance licked her lips and overacted a seductive routine towards me. After they'd had their fun and calmed down again, Self-Importance changed to a more ladylike position and added her input to our discussion.

Self-Importance: "Intimate relationships that are based solely on the concepts of friendship are not likely to work well here, Richey, because it is unlikely they will be accepted. Jealousy, Betrayal, Suspicion, Infidelity, myself, and others have a very tight grip on this world, and it is not likely that the majority of people will become aware enough of us to give us much thought, let alone reject us out of hand for the likes of Friendship. Let's face it, honey, seduction is a lot more fun, and emotionally charged when the threat of infidelity, betrayal, and jealousy are a part of it. We own this world and I don't see any of us giving it up any time soon."

Jealousy: "That's telling' him, babe (she bangs on a table with her hand and repeats herself). You tell him!"

Divorce: "*She's right, Richard, we're here to stay and it's not likely we'll leave in the next few millennia either.*"

Me: (Acting undaunted) "*That may be so, but that doesn't mean that I and others like me can't leave this world for another world where Friendship rules supreme and most of you are only memories.*"

Self-Importance: "*Don't kid yourself, Richey; I have an iron clad grip on the majority of the humans in this world, and you personally know all too well how difficult it is to break my hold.*"

Me: "*I remember when I was a boy in church and I read that passage in the New Testament where Jesus' disciples asked him if there was marriage in heaven. Do you remember what he said?*

A chorus of voices respond: "*Yeah, yeah, we remember, we were all there when he said it; so what?*"

Me: "*When I was a boy I was very curious as to why Jesus said there was no marriage in heaven and I quizzed my father about it. If marriage was so great and sacred as the church led us to believe, then why wouldn't it exist in heaven? But the better I have gotten to know all of you I can certainly see why this is so.*"

Romance: "*Ha! They all know why too, but they don't want to admit it. Heaven wouldn't be heaven and a place of peace if all of these jokers could exist there.*"

Jealousy: "*We have already found our heaven.*"

Self-Importance: "*And it is right here where we rule and feed off of you.*"

"Of the delights of this world man cares most for sexual intercourse, yet he has left it out of his heaven."
~ Mark Twain ~

PART TWO:
THE NEW TESTAMENT

FRIENDSHIP:
THE NEW DEAL

"My life is my message."
~ Mahatma Gandhi ~

The ability to perceive the boundaries of a new world, then turn and step into this novel realm is the core material of myth and legend. In the following chapters, however, we will attempt to identify the physical boundaries of this new, mythical land and then discuss the pragmatic possibilities of traversing into it and actually existing there. But what does this world look like and how will we know it? And what is the key to the magic that makes the world stand still long enough so we can turn and step into it and experience it directly?

It may be difficult to identify something that is only an idea to most of us, but for me this new world is as real as anything a person can lay his eyes, hands and feet upon. So the only real difficulty is giving a reasonable description of something that others may have no experience with. How does one, for example, describe a trip to the moon and a walk on the lunar surface to someone who has never experienced space travel and less than normal gravity?

Well, I would suggest that one should simply shut off his preconceived notions and take a walk with me on the other worldly side of romance and intimacy that we'll come to know as friendship. Because the possibilities for the types of connections we want with women are endless, and the number of women who are already there waiting on guys like us are just as infinite as the universe is wide.

> *"We must be willing to get rid of the life we've planned,*
> *so as to have the life that is waiting for us."*
> *~ Joseph Campbell ~*

7
Book Seven:
THE MARK OF CHANGE

"One must never lose time in vainly regretting the past
nor complaining against the changes which cause us discomfort,
for change is the very essence of life."
~ Anatole France ~

Okay, let's forget all of the stuff we've learned about romance and intimacy for just a moment and let us think about one or two of our very closest male buddies. What are the differences in the way we treat and view them from the way we treat and view our women? Do we worry and fret about them when they are not around? Do we wonder and worry about who they are sleeping with if we haven't seen them in a few days? Do we get upset if they don't call us immediately when we leave them a message or when they don't call every day to check in? Do we have the need to tell them how to dress, how to act, where to go, who they can see, and who they cannot see, or who they can or cannot be friends with? Do we drive by their houses to see if they have company we don't know about and to see if they are telling us lies about their activities and whereabouts? Do we lose sleep when one of them tells us he has a new lady, and do we stress out when we think he may be seeing his new lady as much or more than he sees us? Do we become offended and get our feelings crushed when our buddies don't remember our birthdays or the anniversaries of the dates when we first met, or the date of the first Angels'-Yankees' game we attended together? Do we need to constantly paw and cling to our buddies in public? And yet, who remains in our lives steadfastly when our lovers go away?

What is it about us humans that makes us have to suddenly change our behavior and the rules for the "friends" that we happen to be having sex with, or may have sex with? Is it really reasonable to expect such distinctly different treatment and behavior from a friend who happens to be a lover than it is from a friend who is not? Many people automatically believe that this change is a natural part of our instinctual heritage, but I am convinced that this is learned behavior that is dictated principally by the social mind. According to our social mind, the people we have sex with are in an entirely different category of their own, but for me there are few things more frustrating and annoying than women I have made friends with who instantly change the expectations of our relationship and friendship once we have become physically intimate. Arguably men are probably less likely than women to instantly become connected and emotionally vulnerable to the partners with whom we have just been sexual, but we have all been hooked by someone who really caught our attention or who really mattered to us. And the next thing we knew we were calling them, checking up on them, questioning their intentions toward us and then trying to get them to bend to our will. So what makes our social minds want to do this and rule the behaviors of those we have sex with? Could it be remnants of the ten-thousand-year-old Deal that makes us suddenly shift our focus to those we have sex with, and then act as if they are now our personal property because we have had our penises in them? Does the voice of the social mind tell us that all of these people over here are our friends and this person over here is my lover, so now I have some special property rights to the lover that I didn't have before?

If we are practicing or experiencing any of the above control issues or anxieties when we are physically intimate with a woman, then we have already lost in The Deal-making process and are as good as whooped. Keep in mind that *whatever or whoever we attempt to control only ends up controlling us* in the long run. And to illustrate this point, let's imagine for a moment that one is driving in his car and he fixes his eyes on a specific object, such as a road sign or lamppost. As he approaches the object he is looking at and continues to fixate on it as he passes by, he will have to keep turning his head backward until he is completely unable to see where he is going. And if he doesn't break this fixation and look where he is going his progress will surely come to an abrupt and probably unpleasant halt. By fixing our gaze on control, we are simply pulled into the situation and are allowing it to take over our direction and results. When our attention is completely focused on one thing—control—it is unable to adjust as required to avoid the obstacles that cause us to crash and burn.

If we feel like we have to control a love affair or the behavior of a lover, we have in essence given her the power to castrate us at a moment's notice, even if she isn't yet aware of the power we have turned over to her. Because the first time she doesn't do our program, we lose it. And now she has the power to set us off at any time and take our attention and energy from the rest of our lives, even when this is not her intent. I don't mean to imply that one must instantly become the Rock of Gibraltar the first time he is intimate with a new partner. A man should be prepared to work quickly toward the personal resolution that he can only nurture a relationship and can in no way control it. Control is not a basic building block of friendship, and the need to control the life and behavior of a lover is a foolhardy venture that is doomed to utter failure.

"Anything you strive to hold captive will hold you captive
and if you desire freedom you must give freedom."
~ Peace Pilgrim ~

I have met numerous women who prefer to be the dominant partner in sexual relationships with men, but I met one recently who was fairly articulate. Since this type of preference has always fascinated me I asked what motivated her and she responded to me in an e-mail. This is what she said:

"What planet are you from? It has been my experience and that of most of my women friends, that men think they should decide everything and that the world, by rights, ought to revolve around them. Tying a man up is one way of getting him to slow down and actually engage in adequate foreplay. My interests in this area are more complex than that, but I've found out this technique works."

It is clear this woman has been selecting male companions who have a strong need to be in control of all aspects of their relationship with her, or at least this is her perception of them. And, I would naturally assume that her father was probably the first of these controlling men because we all tend to date and marry replications of our parents. So her response is to find men who will let her take charge by allowing themselves to be immobilized and then coerced into engaging in "adequate foreplay'." Apparently she also believes that her idea of "adequate foreplay" should also be the accepted standard by men as well, but I have news for her on this specific issue. To further clarify her image of men, I asked for some specifics and here is what she told me:

"I live in the Bible Belt.

"My father insisted I have his name put on my first bank account when I was in my teens. He also insisted on having a key to my first apartment. And, if I stayed at my parent's house for a visit, he set my bedtime—'Lights out!'

"Some years ago I had a friend who felt she had to ask her husband's 'permission' to cut her hair from shoulder-length to something she found easier to manage with two toddlers and an infant at home. *And* she had to get his permission to get a part-time job so she wouldn't go bonkers!

"I've had boyfriends who 'insisted' on driving, even though we were going in *my* car. One boyfriend screamed at me if I left the house without make-up on. After him, I stopped wearing any make-up except when onstage. I do occasionally wear some now. Numbers of guys have tried to critique my wardrobe. One guy threatened to 'break my neck' if any of *his* friends ever made a pass at me.

"I had one friend whose husband would pinch or slap her if he didn't like what she'd prepared for supper.

"My brother-in-law once stated that he'd make my sister quit any job if she got paid more than he did.

"This is only a short list. I have more examples, but I'm saving them for when I write a book."

In the end, women only want to escape men who attempt to impose these measures of control on them. I remember more than twenty years ago when I became a complete and total moron myself by trying to control a love affair that was already deeply flawed, but that I was still insecure about losing. My insecurities became so prominent that I couldn't focus on anything else at the time and when the affair finally collapsed, it did so in a sudden and painful crash. Looking back I can easily see that all she wanted was for me to get my composure back and to act like the secure, detached, and confident man she fell in love with. But my feelings of hurt and being out of control were so overwhelming that all I could do was to write her an offensive letter that told her how horrible I felt she had been to me. Geeesh, it almost nauseates me even now to remember what a total lunatic I had become when I felt I had lost control over the direction of this affair. And of course, all I could think to do was try to continue to control her by making her feel guilty with an odious letter.

She wasn't Catholic, but she was Jewish, and we all know about those two kinds of guilt. I should have known, however, that I couldn't be as good at dishing out the guilt as her mother and father were. It probably took me a good three weeks to be able to get a good night's sleep after we split the sheets, but luckily there was a fortuitous and wonderful event that did occur as a result of my foolish behavior.

"The only real mistake is the one from which we learn nothing."
~ John Enoch Powell ~

****

I had planned a month-long visit to China before these interviews were under way so I could visit friends and investigate some potential business opportunities. I am not exactly certain why I enjoy being in China and Asia so much, but I like to go whenever I have the chance. Therefore, it seemed only natural to continue with the interviews while I enjoyed the Chinese countryside and culture. My trip would take me all over the country, but I was going to base myself in Hong Kong, so I invited my Inorganic guests to first meet me at the waterfront Garden City Hotel in the area of the city known as North Point. The view across the bay from the twenty-eighth floor is spectacular and I can never get enough of it. When the Inorganics showed up to meet with me they had all changed their appearance to look as if they were Asian. Self-Importance and Monogamy were their usual seductive and beautiful selves.

Self-Importance: "So, Richey, trying to be cheap again? What are you paying per night here, $150 to $175? You know you could have upgraded to a nicer and bigger room in another hotel for only an extra $100 to $200 per night? There is another place over by..."

Me: "I like this place." (I interrupted her to change the subject.)

Self-Importance: (Looking for something else to harass me with) "Are you going to tell your readers about the time that Jewish chick Diane dumped you really hard? My goodness, you were a mess."

Me: "Yeah, I thought I would mention it. As you know, I made an important decision that changed me dramatically as a result of that fiasco."

Romance: "Oh yeah, I remember that incident. (He looks at me and gestures with his finger toward the Asian Self-Importance.) That was the very first time you decided to break things off with the Asian cutie here."

Divorce: "You had to know the relationship with that Diane chick would never work though? I mean, my god, Richard, she was such a replica of your mother."

Jealousy: "Well, I liked her and I think she was good for you. There weren't too many women who could make you as jealous as she certainly did. And I like women who can make you cocky guys give in to me. It gives me great pleasure to bring you overconfident bastards down a few notches."

Jealousy, Monogamy and Self-Importance let out a short burst of belly laughter.

Marriage: "I liked her too, because I could tell you might have married her, even if it was just to tie her down and to make yourself feel like you had control. She was a bright, well-educated professional and she kept you on your toes."

Monogamy: "Ditto. You turned into a fairly monogamous man while you were with her and she didn't even demand it."

Jealousy: *"You know you were just afraid that she would have stomped on you in the long run, though. In fact, the day you moved out she invited an old boyfriend over and slept with him that very night."*

Self-Importance: *"And who was that darling black chick you abruptly dumped because you had so little energy for anything but dealing with Diane?"*

Romance: *"Yes, that poor girl, you had been trying to get in her pants for weeks and when she finally gives into you the first thing you do is dump her for Diane?"*

Marriage: *"Yes, that young woman really liked you too. She would have done anything for you."*

Me: *"I know, I know, Jenny was such a sweetheart and a very nurturing person too. The problem was that she had an opening in her life for someone who wanted to be loved, but I was too busy trying to fill this role in the life of a woman who didn't really have the same vacancy. I was an idiot and I have kicked myself numerous times over that one."*

<u>*Romance:*</u> *"I have witnessed this same behavior in all of you humans over the centuries and to no end. <u>You people are constantly walking away from others who are absolutely dying to love you, and all because you don't feel exactly the same in return, or didn't feel the chemistry thing when you met."</u>*

Self-Importance: *"The real problem for most of you is that you don't feel like you deserve to be loved like that, especially if you don't think you feel exactly the same in return. Geeesh, what a waste."*

Romance: *"Well, if you wouldn't have run off to the Virgin Islands you could have had her back. In fact, Jenny waited months for you to call her and would have gone down to St. Croix to be with you."*

Jealousy: *(In mocking fashion and elongating the word introspective) Naaah, he was too busy disappearing into his introspective side."*

Self-Importance; "That's right! He sat on his bed, still stinging from his defeat with Diane mind you, and promised himself that he would learn to love women openly and freely so he could just enjoy them without having to feel destroyed when things didn't go the way he wanted."

Me: "And?"

Monogamy: (Looking at Self-Importance) "Well, you gotta admit, babe, he has done a pretty good job of it."

Self-Importance: (Rolling her eyes and looking unimpressed) "Oh, I suppose."

Jealousy: (Looking at Self-Importance and genuinely surprised) "You suppose! Hell, the guy is a walking billboard for detachment these days."

Monogamy: "I think he is just afraid of abandonment."

Self-Importance: "Yeah, Richard, what an asshole you have become. You are no fun at all. I liked you much better when we could easily jerk your chain and make you respond the way we liked."

Monogamy: "I still think this concept of sexual intimacy with friends is totally weird. The very nature and dynamics of the relationship is supposed to change with physical intimacy."

Me: "This is the very reason people struggle with marriage, because they can't imagine a sexual relationship with someone who is a friend. So they marry people who aren't friends and with whom they place totally unrealistic expectations."

Jealousy: "What a self-cleansing and self-healing experience this must be for you, Richard. You are just trying to convince yourself, other men, and women too that you have a better way."

**"The greatest discovery of my generation
is that human beings can alter their lives
by altering their attitudes of mind."
~ William James ~**

8
Book Eight:
THE ACTS OF
DETACHMENT

"Better indeed is knowledge than mechanical practice.
Better than knowledge is meditation.
But better still is surrender of attachment to results,
because there follows immediate peace."
Bhagavad-Gita

From the very beginning of our lives, and under the direct supervision of the Inorganics, the social mind is installed and programmed to take over and then tell us what is what. And one of the primary functions of this social mind software is to measure the amount of sustenance we are providing the Inorganics. All of us are taught from birth to pay attention to the immediate response we get from others and then calculate this response to see if it is given at an acceptable level and frequency. When we start dating someone, living with someone, or we marry someone, one of the primary ways we measure their love and affection for us is by watching the way they respond to our feelings, moods, and requests. If they don't respond and acquiesce to our pleas for specific actions or to our admonishments for change the way we think they should, then we often move to protect ourselves and frequently to punish the offender by withdrawing our affection.

Part of the social mind installation process occurs as children when we are either punished or rewarded by the direct response we give to those adults in authority over us. If Johnny brings home a bad report card he is banished to his room and grounded until he brings home a report card that indicates he is conforming to expectations. And, if he doesn't show the proper remorse for his academic heresy it is an indication that he does not share the authority's morals and values, so other forms of consequences such as corporal punishment may result as well. If he does eventually come home with improved academic marks his sentence is most often reduced or commuted and he is likely to get his television and telephone returned and he can come out of his room when he likes. So unless the consequences are well established and the parent is very savvy with nonjudgmental implementation the implied message to the child's mind is this:

"If you are what I want you to be, I will give you love, affection and acceptance. If you are not the person I want you to be, I will withhold my love and affection and will punish you until you become the person that I prefer."

Children are not good at separating inappropriate behaviors from their person, but neither are most adults. When we tell a child that he or she "is bad" or is "being bad," the child doesn't understand that we are referring specifically to the inappropriate behavior and not to his or her self-worth. So children most often hear, "I'm a bad person," and then they form this self-image, which usually evolves into a self-fulfilling prophecy. One of my former sixth-grade special education students informed me that his grandmother told him frequently that "the devil is in you, boy," so he didn't see why he should have to behave. Since grandma had already declared that he wasn't capable of appropriate behavior it didn't seem reasonable to him that I would hold him accountable to a higher standard. He said he wanted to behave for Grandma, but it was too much work and he got more attention when he misbehaved, even though the attention was negative. If Grandma would give him as much attention for behaving as she did for misbehaving, then he might consider this a viable option. Therefore, we train children to measure our love and affection for them by their willingness to change and give us what we want. And they counter this training strategy by measuring what we are willing to do for them.

I was at a school site a few years ago and became involved in the discussion of consequences with an eleven-year-old boy who had hit another student. When the discussion was nearly over and I was left alone with the boy, he picked his words carefully and said, "Mr. Mills, when I hit another kid I get into trouble, but when my parents hit me they say they are doing it because they love me, so it must be okay to only hit the people you love?"

Now I honestly don't mean to imply that we shouldn't have strategic and suitable consequences for our children when they don't behave appropriately or don't meet agreed upon standards of performance. Teaching children to take full responsibility for themselves and their actions is a vital strategy to rearing emotionally healthy, stable, happy, and successful young adults. But skillful delivery and nonjudgmental consequences are vital to healthy guidance. And without ever realizing what we do to our children, we demonstate the unconscious, subtle, common and uninhibited practice of measuring their response to us, and then we dole out our love and affection to them in subjective proportion. And we demonstrate this process to our children throughout their childhood, over and over again, until their conduct meets our perceived notions of appropriate choice-making. Then, our software social mind begins to kick in automatically without realizing exactly what we are doing, and we carry this measurement and subsequent doling out process from our childhood into our adult worlds. When we meet someone we really like as an adult and our social mind programming takes over, we assume it is our true feelings that are being hurt when someone doesn't measure up.

How many times have we heard this expression when a lover wanted us to change our behavior to suit her needs or preferences: "If you really loved me you would...(or wouldn't)?" And as a result we often do alter our behavior, at least temporarily, to meet this challenge. But the message this expectation relays is this: "I want you to be something other than what you are, just for me, so I can measure your love by a standard I understand." Then after days, weeks, months, or years, we often end up resenting the changes we were forced into making and we resent the person who "made us" make them. Accepting someone else's standards is one thing, but agreeing to own and live by them indefinitely is quite another.

> *"Example is not the main thing in influencing others.*
> *It's the only thing."*
> *~ Albert Schweitzer ~*

When I was six years old and in the first grade, my family lived in a mobile home park in North Topeka and I could easily walk or ride my bike the three or four blocks to school by myself. I usually took my own lunch, but those little half-pints of milk were a nickel at the school cafeteria in those days and my father would usually leave or give me the milk nickel each morning before I departed. On many occasions, however, I would stop by the corner drug store instead, which was right along the way, and would spend my milk money on a little plastic ring for Maria Elena Rodriquez. Then I would wait until no one was looking in our classroom and I would leave the ring on her desk. I used to love to watch her find it and then look around the room for anyone she could suspect. Eventually though, my affection for the little cutie was not something I could hide any longer, so I finally had to make my intentions clear to her. And much to my delight, Maria Elena was willing to return my affection, and we quickly became an item.

Everywhere Maria Elena and I went we did so arm in arm or hand in hand, and I felt truly blessed by my good fortune. It was one of my first major attempts in life to achieve a goal that really mattered to me and the result was a resounding success! What a great confidence builder this little experience was for me at that time and what a serious little cutie I had captured. My good fortune was capped every day by the warmth of her smile and reinforced by her soft touch and adoring gaze. Who knew at ages six and seven that love could be such a pleasant and emotionally rewarding experience? And then, of course, it had to happen. Some little boy named Larry moved in across North Topeka Boulevard from me and immediately locked his sights on my little cutie.

Everywhere Maria Elena and I went there was Larry, following us, butting in, and horning in on my good fortune. He became such an omnipresent fixture that eventually when Maria Elena and I walked arm in arm or hand in hand somewhere, I would find Larry on the other side of her also walking arm in arm or holding her other hand. Naturally, I knew that this couldn't go on indefinitely, so Larry and I decided to act one day and on the back steps of the school we confronted our little girlfriend and demanded that she choose between us.

I remember clearly the contemplative look on her cute little face as she gently bit her lip, looked us over, and then finally made her decision. I even remember my inner feelings and emotional response as she wrapped her lovely little arms around Larry's neck and looked at me sheepishly to show me that she had made her choice, and that it wasn't me. As an adult, one would likely assume that I was probably crushed and that I felt let down and betrayed, because this is the response that most of us have learned; but in truth, this wasn't at all the case. Since my parents were still very young, close, and highly affectionate with one another, I had never witnessed much jealousy, doubt, or feelings of betrayal, so I couldn't even relate to these responses at the time. What I did feel, however, was a new sense of instant challenge, and the thought that "this will never stand" went immediately through my head. I felt bold, daring and determined, as if I had been given a new challenge in life to which occasion I knew I could certainly rise.

Fortunately, I spent no time or energy at all wallowing in self-pity because I had not yet learned this response to disappointing love affairs. So no time at all had passed by before I found another cute little girl to focus on and the whole milk money ring thing started all over. Hey, it had worked quite well before and it worked again this next time too. And it was my detachment from the concerns of failure and loss that allowed me to quickly move on to the new experience and accomplishment.

"The people who get on in this world
are the people who get up and look for the circumstances they want,
and, if they can't find them, make them."
~ George Bernard Shaw ~

It was several years later before I realized that my response to Maria Elena's rejection was inappropriate to the Inorganics and to the operation of social mind software. I was going to Crane Junior High School then and I had asked a round-faced little cutie to dance with me at a school "sock-hop." And much to my delight, she not only danced with me, she nearly made love to me on the dance floor to let me know that she was interested in a lot more than just a foot trot around the gymnasium. Again, I was certain I had hit the jackpot and was being rewarded by God for being the good person I truly was. Wow, what luck! All I did was pick a girl who I was fairly certain would accept my dance invitation and then she took it upon herself to let me know that she was more than pleased that I was paying attention to her. I went home that night buzzing with joy and anticipation, not to mention the rock hard erection I had for the entire weekend that followed. And then, of course, like a bad dream, it had to happen again.

Before this little cutie and I could even get started I was walking home with some of my buddies the following week. I had seen my new little friend at school the past couple of days and we had exchanged warm smiles, a few little touches, and looks of "just wait until I get you alone." But on my walk with my buddies this particular afternoon we caught a glimpse of my new friend walking home in the company of another boy that I knew to be her neighbor. I waved to her casually so my buddies wouldn't harass me for being "pussy whipped" and smiled to let her know I was glad to see her. And then, from out of nowhere, the Inorganics showed up and took over my buddies' voices and bodies:

Envy: "Damn, Mills, are you gonna take that shit?"

Me: "What shit?"

Self-doubt: "Your new squeeze, man!"

Envy: "Yeah, you just hooked up with that bitch and she is already walking home with some other guy."

Me: "The guy is her neighbor."

Self-doubt: "Fuck that!"

Envy: "I wouldn't take that shit, not from any chick, I don't care who the guy is."

Me: "Oh come on, it's no big thing."

Envy: "Yeah, that's what you think. And you're a fool if you think that shit is okay."

Self-doubt: "Besides, you ever see where that chick lives? I don't think she has the best hygiene either. She has kind of a feminine odor that's not good."

I was stunned by the appearance of these beings. How could they just take over my buddies like that? And how could I continue my new love affair with this girl if I had to keeping facing these creatures and be harassed by them? Their appearance was so unpleasant that I couldn't imagine dealing with them on any regular basis, so I made an unconscious decision to avoid them if possible. The Inorganics' conditioning had begun with a full scale assault and to fend them off I started ignoring the sweet little girl the very next day.

And I did such a good job of ignoring her that she never ever talked to me again.

"We either make ourselves miserable,
or we make ourselves strong.
The amount of work is the same."
~ Carlos Castaneda ~

Detachment is probably the only way to free one's self from the social mind and become aware of the normally unconscious and powerful influence of the Inorganics. Detachment is what athletes use when they are facing their event's last performance test and must execute a perfect and flawless set of maneuvers to take the gold medal or win the championship as a team. It's what fighter pilots and soldiers must use in combat to keep their wits about them and kill the enemy before the enemy kills them. It is the mood and the face that policemen and firemen must wear daily to keep their cool when confronted with dangerous circumstances and the high odds of being inflicted with great bodily harm. And it is the only way we humans have to recognize the Inorganics as they really are, and to make practical, well thought-out decisions to either reject or accept their influence. This doesn't mean that we don't care about others or how others feel. In fact, it serves just the opposite purpose and frees us up to love and to feel at a much deeper level than we ever thought possible because we are no longer busy giving into our fears, doubts and concerns of failure. By learning to detach ourselves from the petty jealousies and customary anxieties of the average world, we free ourselves to pursue our dreams with a gusto that is not available to the average man.

There is no room in one's life for joy, security, self-determination, confidence and success when fear, worry, doubt and failure are consuming the person's energy. And probably the most self-defeating of these Inorganics are self-importance and self-pity, which are those constant, nagging, complaining, whining inner voices that tell us we are being had, used, betrayed, abandoned, cheated, lied to, overlooked, bypassed, and taken for a ride, etc. It is the inner voice of self-importance that is the most common source of bitter, nasty, vicious divorces where each party is more deserving and entitled than the other to the cash, investments, property, business and children. And it is this inner voice of self-pity that convinces us that our cheating, inconsiderate, hateful, ungrateful, conniving lover has used and abused us in unspeakable ways and that we have the right and the honor-bound duty to resent them.

Self-importance is the primary instigator and ongoing facilitator of war, murder, execution, suicide bombing, terrorism and invasion because each perpetrator has to believe that his or her view of the world is the only correct view, and that only he or she can have the corner on truth and justice. And self-pity is the primary element that self-important people use as an empathetic connection to the downtrodden and deserving, so the violent perpetrator can find justification for the acts of brutality and cruel carnage that he or she commits.

As long as the negative Inorganics rule relationships and marriage, you can bet that divorce will continue to increase from the current sixty percent rate it has now climbed to and that divorce will continue to be the nasty, rough and tumble affair that is has become. And the people who continue to blame divorce for the harm it causes children are only kidding themselves; because the mature, confident grownups who accept that people sometimes part company will rear children who do not create bitter, debilitating endings to love affairs.

"Friendship renders prosperity more brilliant,
while it lightens adversity by sharing it
and making its burden common."
~ Marcus Tullius Cicero ~

****

While I was hanging out in Hong Kong I decided to take the train-tram up to Victoria Peak so I could have a leisurely lunch while I overlooked the magnificent city of high rises below. There are huge patios up there to dine on and plenty of room, so I expected the Inorganics to join me and they did:

Self-Importance: "Oh god, more take-out food. Let's go to a real restaurant."

Romance: "Hey, Richard, I see why you like it up here. What a great place to bring a date."

Jealousy: "Yeah, and we are his dates. What a lucky guy."

Monogamy: (With a devious smile) "See, Richard, I'm flexible and willing to share you with others."

The rest of them let out some laughter.

Me: (Sincere and contemplative) "I really don't have a problem with you, Serial Monogamy, as long as people choose you because of a well thought-out personal choice, and not because of some bullshit moral expectation imposed on men by the self-anointed moral police, who then expect to bully us into kowtowing to you or be labeled as incorrigible assholes, pigs and dogs."

Self-Importance: (Leaning over to catch my eyes and to look sincere) "So Richey, how do you really feel, honey?"

The rest of them let loose with some snickering.

Monogamy: "Hmm, a little male self-persecution here?"

Self-Importance: "Richey honey, you really have to be kidding yourself to think your male readers are going to be able, or even willing, to break the hold we have on them and to start building friendships with women above all, else. Lust, Greed, Envy—these are all very powerful Inorganics and forces in the lives of your fellow men."

Divorce: "And as long as I am an option, I don't see the motivation for people to change. Besides, I'm not all that crazy about the idea of men being able to significantly improve their intimate relationships with women and make them more enduring anyway."

Me: "I hate to burst your bubble, gang, but if I can do it, so can millions of other men. And when men are sick and tired enough of giving away their personal power and their wealth, they are very likely to climb on board."

Monogamy: "Now you sound like a victim."

Marriage: "And you think that letting people design marriage contracts the way that best serves their purpose as a couple is a good way to fix me?"

Me: "I think that people have to evolve sooner or later when something isn't working, and clearly marriage as we've known it is no longer working. One doesn't have to be a scientist or genius to see this."

Monogamy: "I strongly disagree."

Me: (To Monogamy) "How many times did you say you've been married and divorced?"

Marriage: "Then maybe it would be prudent to go back to the more conservative and traditional values that made marriage great and the lifetime bond that it once was?"

Me: "I know of a lot of die hard conservative, religious, and political leaders who would certainly agree with that premise, but it's not going to happen like that, especially with the current rate of life expectancy growing as it is and with prenuptial agreements becoming more common."

Self-Importance: "Don't be too sure about that. Just take a look at your own country these days. Those die hard moral police have been pretty successful at reversing popular trends. Consider what happened after Janet Jackson showed her lovely boob at the Super Bowl Halftime Show. Those moral police went berserk, didn't they?"

Me: "Yeah, can you believe that? It's okay to show dead bodies blown to bits and littering the streets of the U.S. after a disaster and to show bodies littering the streets in Iraq, Haiti, Afghanistan, Israel and Rwanda after bombs, gun fights; and genocide; but show a little boob on prime time television and people go ballistic. Is that kind of thinking a bit warped, or is it just me?"

Divorce: "We don't care."

Me: "Oftentimes we Americans appear to be more offended by life and sensuality than we are by violence and destruction."

Marriage: "Self-Importance is right, Richard, change is very slow to come and there are always setbacks."

Me: "Maybe, but there are too many signs that permanent change is here to stay and that more are on the horizon."

Jealousy: "Such as?"

Romance: "The ones he discussed before. Prenuptial agreements are not going away and are only likely to increase in numbers and scope. Gay marriages have been occurring by the thousands in several cites across the U.S.; the divorce rate is running about sixty percent and climbing; people are waiting longer and longer to get married; more and more people are not getting married at all; no fault divorce is easy to get; the news is full of people taking their wealthy spouses to the cleaners; and people still give into jealousy, anger, hurt, infidelity and revenge by the millions." (Proudly smiling at me) "So, how'd I do?"

Me: (I give Romance a nod of approval) "Up until the 1920s the average length of marriage was fifteen years and the average number of marriages was three mostly likely because of the mortality rate. In 1982 a book titled Singles: The New Americans, *was published and it had some interesting research data. For example, the researchers surveyed couples from all ethnic backgrounds and social classes that had been married for fifty years or more, and you know what their most significant finding was?"*

Monogamy: "Tell us, we're dying to know."

Divorce: "Well, I am!"

Me: "They found that all of the couples who had been married for fifty years or longer still had the same problems after fifty years that they all had when they first got married. In fact, the findings depressed the researchers so much they had to start canceling appointments to allow more recovery time between the interviews of these couples."

Divorce: (Smiling to himself) "Kewl."

Monogamy: "There is no problem-free life or relationship."

Me: "If people really wanted to stay married for fifty years or longer you all know they would have to detach themselves from you completely, because we all know what attachment to you means."

Monogamy: "Yeah, you wish."

Jealousy: "Fuck 'em, I'm not letting people go, no matter how many marriages they have to go through."

Self-Importance: "Me either! I don't give a rat's ass about the length of marriage or even if marriage survives as we know it. All I care about is my own survival and ruling people's lives for eternity."

Marriage: "We are too important and godlike to most people, Richard, so there is no way they can detach themselves from us in significant numbers just because you and a few others have."

Jealousy: "You know that most people don't see us and converse with us like you do. They believe our voices are their own inner thoughts and they just turn themselves over to us when certain stimuli or suspicions arise, no matter how ridiculous they may be. When someone believes he has the right to become jealous, he is thoroughly trained to think of me as his own inner feeling and reaction. It's a great gig, and as you know we have been highly successful at it for eons."

Self-Importance: "People are going to think you have multiple personalities if you try to convince them of our existence, Richey."

Monogamy: "People see detachment as a survival mechanism only and not something that is meant to be a permanent state of mind, so they'll never see or acknowledge us."

Romance: "I don't know, I think people are becoming more and more sophisticated and I have a feeling that Richard here is only a harbinger of things to come."

Monogamy: "I think his book will only appeal to the males like Richard who have a self-persecuted victim attitude and have come out of very unhealthy relationships they chose and don't want to take responsibility for."

Self-Importance: "Sounds like our kind of guys."

Jealousy: "Yes, they do."

Monogamy: "Well, if Richard is at all correct about coming change, how does that affect me?"

Romance: "It means that people are eventually going to give up on Jealousy, Self-Importance, Divorce, Serial Monogamy, and the rest of us here, at least in the form they've always known us, and stop letting all of us run their lives."

Jealousy: "Ha! Over my dead body they will!"

Romance: (Smiling widely) "That's the idea, you old broad, that's the idea."

**"We cling to our own point of view,
as though everything depended on it.
Yet our opinions have no permanence;
like autumn and winter, they gradually pass away."
~ Chuang Tzu ~**

9
Book Nine:
THE EPISTLE OF
PERSONAL HISTORY

"Great people aren't those who are happy
at times of convenience and contentment,
but of who they are in times of catastrophe and controversy."
~ Martin Luther King, Jr. ~

I think my father, Richard Sr, has one of the best examples of a marriage based on the principles of friendship that I have witnessed. His wife Susan is a very attractive brunette who is twenty-three years his junior, and the love she harbors for him is blatantly obvious. My sister Vicky is only seventeen years younger than our father and I am only nineteen years younger, so I'll let everyone do the math for themselves. And even though there is a major difference in my father's and Susan's ages, there is no question to anyone who knows them well that first and foremost they are good friends. I am not sure it was always this way because I didn't live nearby when they started dating, but after twenty years of marriage I have certainly been around them enough to know they are truly buds. After thirty years of life with my mother, my father struggled to learn what emotional baggage belonged to him and what belonged to someone else, so he is very quick to catch himself now when he begins to feel offended or otherwise bothered by something his wife says, doesn't say, does, or doesn't do. We have had several conversations in past years about this topic when he has used me as a sounding board to help him identify and rid himself of past garbage. There is no doubt in me that my father works diligently to approach the issues of his marriage from a fresh point of view and without the burdensome, predestined outcome that personal history produces.

To act consistently in such a fashion takes dogged determination and unbending commitment to the process, as one can imagine, and my father only seems to get better and better at it with each passing year. Although my sister Vicky and I were well into our adult years and Vicky already had two boys when my father and Susan married, they decided to start a family of their own. At first my father told her "no," that he wasn't interested in having more children because he had already reared his children and had two grandsons by the time they married. But Dad eventually changed his mind, and subsequently his future, when he finally realized it was history that was actually saying "no" and making his decision for him. Now I have two young brothers at home and I couldn't be more delighted to be a part of their young and exciting lives.

Personal history is something we all carry with us and it is an incredibly powerful force in our lives that must be reckoned with. Because what would we be without our experiences and the information that it gives us? From age zero to whatever age we are today, we can confidently say that we are the sum total of all that we have endured. If we think about it a moment we will realize that we have no readily retrievable memories from a time that is outside of our current life experiences. And through my college psychology classes and subsequent counseling practices, I have learned that our love patterns are generally set in stone by the age of three, or five at the latest, which is a time that is generally outside of our normal memory retrieval abilities. So our experience is not only a powerful force in making our decisions for us, it is also a subtle, unconscious, and forceful part or our social minds that works either for or against us through subterfuge. It sprouts from deeply embedded roots that were grown long before we had the chance to realize what was occurring to us.

When I was in the third grade my parents purchased their first home that was attached to the ground and moved us out of the trailer park. Having my own larger room and larger closet was certainly a treat, but I was always concerned about the monsters that lived under my bed. When I would turn out the lights at night by the door I would always run across the room to my bed and would dive in before the monsters could reach out and grab me. I am not certain why I felt safe after I was in the bed, but for some reason I felt that I had reached a safety zone and could rest peacefully because I was then out of their grasp.

I carried the memory of the three years we lived in that house into my adulthood and would occasionally relate the story of the monsters under my bed to friends and clients with children. But I never understood the basis of my fears or why I was so certain there were monsters lurking under my bed who were just waiting to get me. Then one day around the age of forty I overheard my mother telling a relative about my teenaged uncle who lived with us when I was very young. She told the relative about how my uncle used to hide under the bed when I was age two or three to scare the hell out of me when I came near.

"We choose our joys and sorrows long before we experience them."
~ Kahlil Gibran ~

Many years ago I was sitting on the sofa next to my girlfriend Tawny, who was tiny in comparison to most people, let alone to me. I am six-foot two-inches tall and was about two hundred twenty pounds back then, but I don't think she is more than four-foot-eleven and ninety pounds soaking wet. Little as she was in those days, she still had a killer body, so her size never deterred me much in any way. While we watched television together we were having a disagreement and I remember she said something that was absolute total nonsense, so I barked loudly at her and turned my large frame sideways to give her a confrontational look of disapproval. As I turned toward her she cowered away from me, ducked her head, and raised her arms to cover her upper torso, as if to protect herself from a pending blow that might be coming from me. But I think my sudden look of surprise at her reaction to me caught her off guard, as much as her protective maneuver caught me off guard, and she quickly said, "I thought you were going to hit me."

I just sat there stunned as I wondered how on earth she could ever think that I would do such as thing as assault her. I told her that she had known me for more than a year and that I had never even come close to that kind of behavior, so I was flabbergasted by her unwarranted assumption. But Tawny continued to justify her fear of being struck, no matter what I said or did. I didn't know what to say to her when she continued to argue her position, and I was totally bewildered by the entire incident. I thought about it for several weeks and decided that even though I was not a violent person I had indeed learned to bully people verbally when I didn't get my way, so I made a conscious commitment to cease that type of behavior. Even though I decided to fix me and not her, I knew her history with her father and ex-husband, so I was fully aware that her response to me was primarily a product of her own history.

In my brief but fascinating tenure as a marriage counselor I witnessed this act of self-projection onto others time and time again from people who were convinced of their significant other's sinister motives; it started more nasty wars between lovers than I am able to recount. So I learned that Personal History doesn't care who we are or what we want and that it is a common Inorganic that only cares about its own existence and power. And Personal History will only do what it must to survive, in spite of any detrimental affect it may have on our human lives.

"We learn from history that we do not learn from history."
~ Georg Friedrich Wilhelm Hege ~

****

A few months after my visit with the Inorganics in Hong Kong I made a month-long trip to Russia. I spent the first several days in Moscow even though I had business elsewhere because I wanted to see some sights and I had tickets to Giacomo Puccini's Chinese opera *Turandot* at the famous and exquisitely beautiful Bolshoi Theater. Russians do love their theater and since I most certainly buy in to the old adage of "When in Rome...," I just had to go. We all know how small to midsize towns throughout the U.S. and Western world have their courthouses or churches in the city center square, right? Well, in Russian towns it is the theater that stands in this place of honor at the center squares and the theaters are usually maintained quite well.

I was early to the Bolshoi Theater so I could have a relaxing dinner across the street in a new shopping center and the Inorganics joined me there. Of course, they had all changed appearance to look like Russians and they spoke English to me with Russian accents.

Self-Importance: "Okay, Richey, I admit that this restaurant is quaint and the woodwork is charming and well-crafted, but it is still a long way from the kind of place you know I would prefer."

Romance: "You like these Russian women, Richard?"

Me: "Sure, they are as gorgeous as any and always impeccably dressed too. Have you noticed?"

Romance: "Many of these women can only afford two or three outfits, but they sure wear them well. And just look at those nice tight little asses. There are almost no fat women among them, especially the younger of them."

Me: "Yes, and tall too. I can't walk more than two or three blocks down the street without passing a number of women who are close to my height or even taller."

Marriage: "You really should consider finding one for a wife, Richard. Matching former Soviet Block women with western men is a huge business now. Didn't your cousin Patrick marry a gorgeous young twenty-something attorney from Romania?"

Jealousy: "Yes, he did, and I was there."

Romance: "What the hell were you doing there?"

Self-Importance: "She goes to all of those weddings to size up future potential and to help facilitate petty family squabbles and jealousies. We both love to be a part of the planning stages because everyone has such big egos and conflicts are easy to start."

Divorce: "See? All I have to do is hang out and wait and these two herd them to me like cattle to the slaughter."

Monogamy: "My favorite is to catch the groom with one of the bride's friends, or vice versa. Even at bachelor and bachelorette parties, everyone tells themselves they have to get one last roll in the hay before they are finally cut off for good. But it never happens that way, because if they cheat then they'll cheat later on for sure."

Me: "So why do you think people make those promises of sexual fidelity when they really don't plan to keep them?"

Romance: "You're kidding, right?"

Self-Importance: "Look, honey, instinct is solely a creation of history, no matter what the nonbelievers think and whether anyone remembers developing it or not. Sure, people can overcome their instincts for a time, but everyone fools around; including animals such as birds, whales, wolves, and numerous other species that pick lifetime mates. When the cat's away, the mice will play; it's a rule of nature across the species."

"We must first find the offense in ourselves
that we perceive as coming from others
if we are to ever free ourselves from its onslaughts."
~ Richard D. Mills ~

Divorce: "You know that the number of married men and women who admit having affairs is roughly seventy percent for each gender. When given assurances of anonymity as many women as men often admit they've fooled around."

Self-Importance: "There are certain species of primates that exist today in the jungles and live in harems with a dominant male, but when a younger, stronger male comes along and the females think he may eventually defeat the older dominant male, they sneak off to have sex with the newcomer. Then, when the newcomer eventually takes over the harem by defeating the old male and running him off, he kills all of the old male's offspring. But he doesn't kill the offspring of the females who had affairs with him because he knows their babies could be his own."

Me: "That's a very sophisticated social structure."

Monogamy: "No joke! And people are no different. Whenever you humans feel threatened, you go out and fool around too. It's simply a part of your survival mode and your history. You have thousands of years of recorded history to see that sexual promiscuity is a deeply imbedded part of your human nature and existence."

Marriage: "A huge issue, of course, is the increased life-span you humans are now having. When you say 'I do' nowadays, you're talking fifty, sixty, maybe even seventy-five years of marriage or more! None of you are really accustomed to this longevity and you're not prepared for it."

Jealousy: (Nodding at Self-Importance) "I have to admit that she and I have something to do with this too. We know people's histories and we love to play on them."

Me: "How so?"

Self-Importance: (Looking annoyed with me) "Don't give me that crap, you smug bastard, you know exactly how we do that. Whenever someone has been betrayed, cheated on, lied to, hurt, abused, abandoned, or whatever, their history opens the door for us to walk right in and make ourselves at home."

"If people can be educated to see the lowly side of their own natures, it may be hoped that they will also learn to understand and to love their fellow men better."
~Carl Jung ~

10

Book Ten:
THE EPISTLE OF INTENT

"Our repeated failure to fully act as we would wish must not discourage us. It is the sincere intention that is the essential thing, and this will in time release us from the bondage of habits which at present seem almost insuperable."
~ Thomas Troward ~

The most important secret a wise man should know about women is a simple formula called friendship. When men truly want to learn to have power in relationships with women and eventually obtain our most coveted favors from them, we must learn first and foremost to view them as friends; because the essence of friendship is the secret to the power and allure they hold over us. I'm not suggesting that we should act like their girlfriends do because this isn't helpful, but there is tremendous power in becoming interested in a woman and who she is: what she believes in, what she likes, where she is from, who her family is, how she feels, what her parents were like, and what she has to say about her day. The most powerful and sophisticated women in the world are highly susceptible to the genuine and sincere interest of a man who doesn't always appear to be after them. And the more beautiful they are, the wiser it is to give virtually no appearance of being after them at all.

To get started we only need to consider the women who are already in our lives, such as the top female executive we see in the hall every day, or the female head of the department or organization where we work, or the consultant who visits our site frequently and offers us advice, or the instructor of the computer course we are taking, or the little old lady who lives down the hall, or the girlfriend of our sister who often comes to visit, or the postal lady who delivers the mail, or our coworkers, fellow students, and even our ex-wives and ex-girlfriends. If we are still wounded novices, we should in the beginning consider the women who pose minimal threat to us and take time to visit with them, ask them about their day and ask them about their dog, their boyfriends, husbands, children, or their work. It is wise to find a woman we can play golf with or with whom we can discuss the business interests that we have in common, and then let our sincerity be the key and glue that keeps the relationship intact. If we try with one and it doesn't work out, we should immediately try another until we can form a bond of trust, mutual respect, and intimacy with a new female friend. And then, when we have been successful with one woman, we need to replicate this success and find another, and then eventually another, and continue to build upon each one until we have collected as many females as we have the time and energy to befriend.

> *"If you want to win a man to your cause,*
> *first convince him that you are his sincere friend."*
> *~ Abraham Lincoln ~*

"WHAT!!! Richard, you must be out of your friggin' mind! I don't even have time for the friends I have now; how can I possibly fit these women into my schedule? And what about my girlfriend; how do I explain these friendships to her? What's the advantage to be gained in having a number of women friends, especially if they are not for sex?"

Making friends with women is the first act in changing the male intent and befriending the Spirit of Womanhood and winning her over to our cause. The Spirit of Womanhood is an Inorganic that we should definitely classify as an angel, because of the positive force she has in the world and the positive force she can be in our male lives. I haven't mentioned this specific Inorganic before, but we can utilize her as a strategic ally when we become aware of the fact that we ally ourselves with certain Inorganics anyway. In the majority of cases, however, the alliances we make with Inorganic Beings is usually an unconscious practice and ploy that often causes us more trouble than we want. As one can imagine, this is a maneuver that requires great caution when trying to ally oneself with any Inorganic, especially an Inorganic that is toxic and of a highly negative nature.

As we befriend more and more women of all ages, shapes, and ethnicities, it is vitally important that we learn to love them without reservation. This conscious endeavor is extremely important because it is a first step that eventually forces us to face our personal histories, which also helps us change our direction to a world and future that will be more satisfying in the long run. If any of these female friends should decide at some point to become sexually interested in us, we should sincerely consider the possibility and then openly share the specific circumstances in which we would be willing to participate in any of the sexual activities we most enjoy. Or, to be as warm and charming as possible when we make it clear that we have no interest in sexual possibilities. The contemporary male will be shocked at some of the things his female friends will be willing to do and share with him once the women feel comfortable with his sincere affection and are comfortable with who he is. Maybe one out of five or one out of ten will be interested in a physical relationship, but when it stems from a solid foundation of friendship and mutual admiration it has a much better chance of enduring.

When we become more and more comfortable with having women as friends and buddies, we can spend more time befriending the types of women who interest and challenge us most, because of their intelligence, beauty, sex appeal, or for any reason that suits our tastes. But make a conscious note that it is a huge mistake to approach a woman friend first for sex, no matter how good she looks and feels, unless she is the one who first broached the topic to the possibility; and even then we cannot get caught up in the conventional pursuit of her for any reason. Another big secret about the female psyche is this: when given a choice between the two, most women would rather love a man passionately than be loved passionately in return. Of course, we would all like to feel that our significant others love us passionately, but when faced with the opportunity, it is more compelling to love this way than to be loved this way. When as males we spend all of our time and energy in blatant pursuit, we set ourselves up for failure and often give our power away by making unacceptable agreements to achieve our sexual goals, and this behavior is no longer acceptable to the bible-toting men who want to take their power back.

In learning how to deal with women the way they have historically dealt with us, <u>through the principles of friendship, we obtain a strategic and commanding advantage</u> in making The New Deal. Women have been incredibly successful in making friends with men and then withholding physical intimacy from them until the guys meet the conditions and criteria the women have established for sexual admittance. But I strongly submit that there is nothing, except the beliefs created by our social minds, to stop us from turning the tables and doing the same thing with women in order to achieve the conditions that we most desire.

> *"The spirit in which a thing is given*
> *determines that in which the debt is acknowledged;*
> *it's the intention, not the face-value of the gift, that's weighed.*
> *~ Seneca ~*

<u>The ability any man has to achieve the conditions he is most interested in having lies solely within his ability to change his intent and then develop his personal power.</u> Take Mr. Hugh Hefner, for example. Now here is a guy who has managed to create the conditions that most of us guys only fantasize about throughout our lifetimes. Sure, he is rich and famous and owns one of the most widely read publications for men in the world, but I can assure everyone

that this didn't happen by accident. Hef is able to maintain several beautiful women as lovers at the same time, and in the midst of a serial monogamous world, mind you, because he had a vision that he focused his energies and personal resources on achieving, and he didn't give up until he was successful. The 1950s was still a very sexually prudish era in the U.S. When Hef started building his dream, the enormous odds and overwhelming moral forces from that time were heavily pitted against him. But in the final analysis it doesn't really matter if these are the same conditions that other men want to achieve or not. Because Hef's example to all of us clearly demonstrates the ability of one man to achieve whatever conditions he wants with the women he is interested in. And those five or six blonde girlfriends that go everywhere with him are drop-dead gorgeous, are they not?

Without intent there is little or no chance that mankind can achieve anything because intent is mankind's direct link to the unlimited forces of the universe that creates all things. When we intend something we automatically align ourselves with its inevitability, and as long as we do not allow doubt to get in the way, we can rest in confidence that sooner or later we will arrive at our choice of destinations. This is how we develop our will and insure that we will be successful at any endeavor we attempt. By clinging doggedly to the powerful force of intent we build an unbending will that becomes the bedrock foundation of our personal power.

"There is only one success.
To be able to spend your life in your own way."
~ Christopher Morley ~

There are very few endeavors that will bring a person more rewards, benefits, and personal power than befriending the spirit of the other gender. And there is little chance that a man will ever be able to fully achieve his intimacy goals with women, whatever they may be, without this course of action. As I stated previously, I don't want to imply that men could ever take the place of his lover's girlfriends, or that he should even try, because this would be a totally futile effort. Men and women have too many enjoyable differences and women need to rely on their girlfriends for the things they don't get from men, and vice versa. But among Western women there is a common problem of thought that translates into an unrealistic expectation that men in the Western world should be just like them.

As I have discussed previously, we have entered an age where women have been highly successful in pushing and legislating their agenda in western societies, and rightly so. But an undesirable and objectionable outcome of this success has been an unreasonable expectation that men should be more like women in how we think, act and feel. Personally, I find this expectation unreasonable at best and I would like to encourage men and women alike to become more aware of the hazards of such thinking. Men don't need to be more like women. What men really need is the liberty to be who we are. Men are not "dogs," "pigs," or "chauvinist assholes" because we think, act and feel differently than women do about certain things that matter more to one gender or the other. Men often fantasize about other women; we often fantasize about numerous partners; we often prefer to get up and go to the fridge, TV, or roll over and go to sleep immediately after sex; and no matter how much women hate this or try to coerce us into other behaviors, this is how the majority of us are made.

"When men and women are able to respect and accept their differences then love has a chance to blossom."
~ John Gray ~

****

After a few days in Moscow, I took the train from the Kazan Station to the city of Yoshkar-Ola, which is the capital of its state, the Mari–El Republic. Yoshkar-Ola is a much smaller city than Moscow with a population of about 150,000 to 170,000 people and is located in west central Russia. I like the place because it reminds me of my hometown of Topeka, Kansas. The Topeka metro area is about 170,000 people and the capital of Kansas, which is about the same size and population of the Mari–El Republic. Trains are not very expensive to ride in Russia so I reserved a two-bed compartment to myself. I had hoped that Friendship would join me for the rest of my discussions with the Inorganics, and as soon as the train was underway, Friendship appeared at my compartment door.

Friendship had always appeared to me as a female Inorganic because of the soft, warm, inviting energy that it emits. So needless to say, I was happy to see her and to have her company on my overnight train ride to Yoshkar-Ola. A couple of days after we arrived we went to the city's premier coffee house named Cappuccinos on the corner of Sovetskay and Gogolya streets in the downtown area. There is only one coffee house like it in Yoshkar-Ola because a three-to-five-dollar order is an expensive affair for the average $50 to $150 monthly wage earners in the area. Friendship and I made ourselves comfortable and the rest of the Inorganics joined us shortly after we sipped down our first order:

Self-Importance: (Dropping herself into a chair with a defeated sigh) "Another coffee house, Richey? My god, man, I know you can do better than this."

Jealousy: (Pointing casually to Friendship with her chin) "So, Richard, I guess you decided you needed some protection?"

Romance: (Smiling broadly) "Not from me, I like his company."

Self-Importance: (Looking pissed, but harmless) "Well, I used to. But he has this untouchable smug attitude now that is really annoying."

Monogamy: "So, Friendship, I take it that you have become one of Richard's closest allies now?"

Friendship: "Absolutely, because who else is going to get him laid?"

They all snicker and chuckle at me.

<u>*Monogamy: "I could get him laid every day, and to anyone he wanted, if he would simply promise to honor me and adhere to my rules and dictates."*</u>

Divorce: "Yeah, I've picked up lots of recently-divorced females who'd love to be with a guy like him too, but too many of them got divorced because Monogamy told them to."

Marriage: "I know dozens of absolutely beautiful women who'd marry Richard in a heartbeat and who would make wonderful wives if he were open to the idea."

Me: "Well, I certainly appreciate the concern and vote of confidence, but I am sure you all know that Friendship and I have a pact, and I find her to be a pretty reliable associate."

Romance: "I like her too. She and I have always gotten along very well." (He looks over at Friendship and winks at her with a smile.)

Monogamy: *"Look, Richard, there is no reason to pull punches or to dance around the facts. We are all painfully aware of the power of intent and the fact that you have learned to hone yours to a fine art. Each of us here has used intent to survive in this world for thousands of years, and we know what it can do, and this is why we agreed to add our two cents to your book. We've seen the results that men like Lao Tzu, Buddha, Jesus, Mohammed, Gandhi and Martin Luther King can get with intent. And even though you are no Jesus, Gandhi or Martin King, we are acutely aware of the door to other worlds that a man like you can open with your intent, so we want to have our say and input before you try to drag other hapless males into your bad dream."*

Jealousy: *(Looking disgusted and standing up to shake her finger at me) "Well, you're not taking any of my food, I can assure you of this. I've worked too damn hard to build my flock over the millennia and you cannot have any of them, you bastard!"*

Self-Importance: *"Oh, chill, girl, he doesn't have the power to influence that many people. There are more than six billion people on this planet and I doubt that he could affect more than a few hundred of them at most…well…maybe a few thousand, tops. Hell, half the people on the planet can't even read, so there are plenty left over for us to breed and replace the handful that he can sway away from us, if he affects any at all."*

Jealousy: *(Acting insulted) "He can't have even one of mine, the son-of-a-bitch. Once that door is open, the assholes just keep flowing through it. In only a hundred years we could lose millions."*

Romance: *(Laughing) "Damn, Richard, if this is the affect you have on women, I'm not sure I wanna throw my hat in with you."*

Me: *"Oh? You'd rather hang around with the likes of her?" (I nodded toward Jealousy.)*

**"Great spirits have always encountered violent opposition
from mediocre minds."**
~ Albert Einstein ~

11
Book Eleven:
HEY JUDE,
ARE WE READY?

"Acquire the courage to believe in yourself.
Many of the things that you have been taught
were at one time the radical ideas of individuals who had the courage
to believe what their own hearts and minds told them was true,
rather than accept the common beliefs of their day."
~ Ching Ning Chu ~

Okay, the bible-toting male is just about ready to set off on his new, personalized journey to obtain the type of relationships he is most interested in achieving with women. And so far, I have given my readers just enough information to get them into serious trouble. So it will be important for everyone to stay tuned for the release of *The Bible For Men: Volume II* when it hits the market. Because there is no doubt that *Volume II* will be needed in the very near future for each man who has actually decided to alter his love life, take his power back, and participate in creating The New Deal with women. Experience is most often the best teacher, but once a man has experienced the impact of directional change and has reached the boundaries of his current road map, he will need another more expansive map that will give him further, more positive directional choices.

So let us now review the pragmatic components of The New Deal and take a look at some additional concepts and explanations that may be very helpful. I want to arm every man as best as possible for his initial journey into this new and unknown territory and do my best to give him something concrete to bolster him on his journey.

✳CHANGE:

Making a decision to seek and to allow change into one's life is without doubt a primary component of human evolution. If we are closed off to change then there is nothing that I or anyone else can do to help another person alter his life and the outcome of his endeavors. Saying "I'm ready for change" out loud to one's self or to another person is the best way to open this door and make it so. Even if it sounds strange or as if it is a weird thing to do, making statements out loud is an effective tool to begin any journey, large or small. How often do we take a journey of any length without first telling someone out loud of our plans, whether a family member, travel agent, paperboy, or postman?

My young cousin and his wife have decided to reconcile and move their little family from Missouri to Minnesota where his mother-in-law lives. He resisted the move originally because he was being threatened with abandonment and divorce if he didn't go along with the program. He told his parents first and when he and I discussed his decision over the phone he said that he knew he was in a rut with his job and living conditions and he had decided that moving might be a good way to jumpstart a new life and get himself out of the doldrums. He listed a number of positive reasons why the move would be beneficial, including a return to school, so I have no doubt that his decision is well-conceived.

After nearly thirty years of living in the same town and working thirteen years at the same school district, my buddy Juan decided to move to another state. I had the feeling he would eventually return, but he said he needed the radical change to get himself out of a rut. He said he socialized with the same crowd, worked with the same crowd, hung out with the same crowd, and needed a new environment where he could meet new people and a whole new set of women. Although he did leave and then moved right back about one year later, he did have a new attitude and he began to meet and befriend new women in the area where he had lived for decades.

These are rather dramatic examples of men who have decided to force themselves into change, but for most of us a move to another state may not be necessary. There are so many things one can do to kickstart a change that the list is far too extensive to catalog here. Nevertheless, I do have a couple of practical ideas to get us started, and my first suggestion is the tactical use of the Internet.

Web sites* that post personal ads have become a very common, mainstream and accepted part of society these days. They connect us to tens of thousands of women we wouldn't otherwise meet, so I hope no one allows themselves to be put off by them. And best of all, these websites allow us to remain fairly anonymous until we decide the time has come to give out our names and contact information to someone we have been corresponding with.

Once a site or two has been selected there is usually a narrative field about oneself that must be filled in. It is in this section where card-carrying, bible-toting men need to express their intent to make friends first, and then participate in physical intimacy if and when our criterion for it is met. It is also wise to experiment here to see what one can say to attract the type of women he is hoping to find. If negative responses are received, simply delete them and do not get caught up in online debates with women who like to fight, because there are plenty of others out there who want to play. It's also wise to beware of women who immediately send their phone numbers, demand that the man call, and then refuse to correspond any further through e-mail. This is usually a control move and a signal that the guy is about to be forced into the pursuit mode and then required to do some chasing. And remember that we *do not* chase anyone to be friends with, because this is not an equitable method in forming lasting friendship bonds and it requires us to surrender a large portion of our power. We don't need women to write us books, but they should be willing to write more than a line or two when responding to our correspondence and questions.

The second idea I want to suggest for the initiation of change is for men to bug their friends and family members for introductions. Something like seventy to eighty percent of all couples who meet and marry are introduced

---

*Please see the last section of this book for web site information and suggestions.

to one another by their mutual friends or by family members. Take the time to meet as many women as reasonably possible and then put energy into the few with genuine friendship potential. After the normal getting to know each other discussion about sex that new couples always have, do not ask or demand sex from any of them and only address the possibility of sex if they appear to be willing to participate in the manner that meets one's preferences. By making friends with women, not asking them for sex, and only then being willing to participate in sexual activity with them under the circumstances *we* set forth, we are effectively changing our direction from one reality to another. It is truly amazing to witness this process firsthand and even more fascinating to witness the behavior of frustrated women who cannot get their way with men by dangling physical affection in front of them like a carrot until the guys comply with their wishes and preferences.

"We must be the change we wish to see in the world."
~ Mahatma Gandhi ~

✗ DETACHMENT:

It is important to set aside some time each week or month to correspond with new women, to meet those women who feel like the best fit, to talk to those women who are the most responsive to our predilections, and to spend time with those women who are the most enjoyable company. It is also vitally important to be prepared to move past those women quickly who want to constantly challenge, debate and criticize our choices for ourselves and for befriending them as we do. As I said earlier, there are a lot of women who like to fight, but engaging them for any lengthy duration is truly a waste of time and energy for the male who wants to build lasting friendships and love affairs. And the only way one can build these lasting relationships effectively is to be free of the need to take offense. As long as we are easily offended by others we will be held captive by them and forced to use our energy to maintain their world and the Inorganics who thrive there.

"The true perfection of man lies, not in what man has,
but in what man is...Nothing should be able to harm a man but himself.
Nothing should be able to rob a man at all. What a man really has is
what is in him. What is outside of him should be a matter of no
importance."
~ Oscar Wilde ~

My grandfather Richard, the first Richard Mills in the series of three, was married to my grandmother for approximately twenty years and had more than half a dozen kids with her. After their marriage went south, my grandfather met his second spouse and started a second family with my step-grandmother Dollie, who was twenty-some years his junior. This woman loved him and took care of him in ways that impressed me to no end, and I loved her too because she was so kind to him and always took such good care of those who were important to him, like me. My grandpa had developed some serious breathing problems after years of smoking and doing arch-welding on the earth movers he maintained for road construction crews, so it was not uncommon for him to be hospitalized in the winter months when he would get a severe cold or flu bug. Grandma Dollie, of course, would be right there to care for his every need. I would always go out of my way to see him when he was hospitalized because I knew he didn't enjoy being there and it was time that we could just hang out together, whether we talked or not. During these visits when he was ill he would always encourage me and my father to find younger women to marry. He would look at me, raise his weathered, leather-skinned finger and say, "Boy! Find you a younger woman and marry her because she'll take care of you when you get old." I used to love to hear that from him and I cannot even begin to express the love, admiration and affection I had for that ornery old guy right up until the day he left this world.

Even with the encouragement and instruction of his father still fresh in his experience, my father had a difficult time getting past his own reservations about marrying a woman who was younger than his own grown children. The only problems I remember my dad and his wife Susan having while they dated were the problems that resulted from his discomfort with their age difference, but it didn't seem to bother Susan at all. My dad is one of those guys who deeply loves to be married and to have a family, because this seems to define him and who he is to a great degree. After many years of holding down two and three jobs at the same time to support us and to rear my sister and me, I was surprised that he would even consider doing it again. But when he finally detached himself from concerns about the judgments and the often vocal condemnation of a few around him, he finally realized that he might never get another chance like this one. And now he has a family that any man would be deeply proud to have and he is living his fondest and most precious dreams.

"If I care to listen to every criticism,
let alone act on them,
then this shop may as well be closed for all other businesses.
I have learned to do my best,
and if the end result is good then I do not care for any criticism,
but if the end result is not good,
then even the praise of ten angels would not make the difference."
~ Abraham Lincoln ~

✳ PERSONAL HISTORY:

It doesn't really matter how many times we have been insulted, lied to, cheated on, betrayed, stomped on, taken to the cleaners, or left: it is simply unacceptable to allow our histories to decide our futures and to recreate the same scenarios for us over and over again, And it's vital that we make it a point to forgive and to forget those who have injured or otherwise offended us in any way and let them go. When people say they are unhappy with their world and the conditions in their lives, just ask them why they don't change it. What we get immediately is a highly practiced and highly polished story about why their world is as it is and why they are unable to change it. Rarely is it their fault their world has developed as it has and rarely is it their fault that it stays the way it has always been.

My sister Vicky is about a year and a half older than me and she is one of the sweetest and nicest people I have ever met. But when we were kids we seemed to fight like cats and dogs, which appears to be fairly typical adolescent behavior between siblings who are close in age. I couldn't even say what we fought over most of the time or why, but I remember some brawls that certainly didn't go my way and I didn't like losing to her one bit. For some strange reason that I couldn't put my finger on I felt that I had to constantly be on guard against her and to watch out for any violation of my rights that she might commit. It wasn't even a conscious thought process that made me act toward her the way I did, but some inner warning bell would ring when I perceived a violation and then I would attack.

Vicky and I grew up with our friends Paula and Gary who had the same age spread between them as we did. But for some reason I didn't become aware of at the time, this brother and sister team got along much better than Vicky and I did. And when I was starting high school I was shocked when I witnessed Paula fixing her brother Gary up with one of her girlfriends. I couldn't believe his good fortune and I couldn't believe his sister would go out of her way to do something so kind for her younger brother. But I was hooked and this act of sisterly match making was the bait that caught me, not to mention the fact that the girl Paula introduced her brother to was a drop-dead gorgeous little fox.

I thought about these two siblings and their affection for each other nonstop over the next few days and I couldn't help but be a little jealous of their bond and warm relationship. And I remember driving home from Paula and Gary's house one day when I decided I would stop my aggressive and combative behavior toward my sister to see if I could change the pattern of war and conflict that we so often found ourselves in. No matter what my grudges were or the resentments I carried for past sins, I decided to release them and to embrace the possibility of a new deal.

Well, the result I almost instantly achieved overnight was astounding, to say the least, and I couldn't believe how nice it was to make a close friend and buddy out of my older sister. But the thing that became the most apparent to me was the fact that Vicky didn't have to make much of an effort at all, because once I ceased my aggressive behavior toward her, the bickering came to an abrupt end. To this day I cannot overlook the fact that it was me all along who kept that sibling rivalry going, and all that I had to do was stop being offended and let it go.

And yes, it wasn't long after this that I found myself smooching intimately on our living room sofa with one of Vicky's girlfriends and it was her girlfriend who had actually initiated the contact. I was too green to really know how to deal with the situation as well as I would have liked, but apparently this girl had become interested in me because she said that my "sister Vicky always had such nice things to say about her brother."

> *"My days of whining and complaining about others have come to an end. Nothing is easier than fault finding...*
> *All it will do is discolor my personality*
> *so that none will want to associate with me.*
> *That was my old life. No more."*
> *~ Og Mandino ~*

 INTENT:

Intent is the foundation for the accomplishment of all things, no matter what they may be. When we set off on a trip, we intend to reach a specific destination, and it is our intent that aligns us with this chosen destination from the very beginning. As we learn to hone and develop our intent it evolves into our will, and our will's strength is directly related to the cleanliness of the link between it and the powers that be in the universe. If we allow doubts and fears to corrupt this link, our will begins to falter and we find ourselves running in circles and living in unpleasant conditions we could be better off without.

I was eighteen when I graduated from Topeka High School. I was well on the way to six-foot-one by then and I weighed around 280 to 290 pounds. I'd like to say that playing football was the reason I had gotten so big in those days, but I know I would have been that big even if I hadn't played at all. By the time I was twenty I had reached six-feet-two-inches and I weighed between 305 to 310 pounds. For several years I had dreamed of going away one day and coming back to surprise everyone with a lean, mean, muscular body and a handsome lean face. I don't remember exactly what age I was when I first focused my attention and awareness on this specific intent, but I remember having it around the age of thirteen or fourteen because I was big even by then.

My bedroom was the center room of the upstairs in the older house we lived in at 1612 Clay and I had these two tall windows that started upwards from near the floor. I slept in the bottom bed of my bunk bed set and the window seals were about parallel to my mattress. It was nice because I could lie there and look down or up and see everything within range of the window. It was here that I formed the intent of going away one day so that I could return a new man, and I would lie there in that bottom bunk and I would stare out the windows and wonder what power would lead me to my destination.

I left for LeTourneau College in Longview, Texas, that fall and worried about my low draft number and what it might be like for a guy like me in Vietnam. The government said they were ending the draft, but the government said lots of things like that and no one ever knew if they meant it or not. I liked Longview okay, but I struggled in the engineering college that required disciplined study skills I had never learned. I worked at a gas station over in Shreveport, Louisiana, on the weekends with my buddy Jim and spent the nights cruising Bossier Strip and wishing I were a lean man who could attract the types of women who attracted me. Although I did have some brief luck with a cutie at school, her availability to me was daunting because I couldn't figure out why she seemed to like me, and I let my fear of looking unattractive scare me away.

Although I knew how to have fun and mostly enjoyed myself, my grades were shit and I couldn't seem to pull myself out of a depression that had begun to set in. My excessive weight was a constant burden on my mind and I couldn't seem to do anything about it, no matter how hard I tried. I loved women and wanted so desperately to date and to have a girlfriend, but my self-image had sunk so low that even when one did show up, I couldn't run away and end it fast enough. After wasting a huge amount of my parent's money during my first try at this private school, I decided to go home to Topeka and try my luck at Washburn University, which is the only city-owned and financed university left in the nation.

I moved into the basement of the new dream house my parents had built while I was away in Texas. The basement had its own entrance and there was a fireplace down there, so I was able to make it my own comfy little domain, even though I knew I couldn't stay there forever. I worked for friends a while pumping gas, but the pay was bad and the hours were long, so when a buddy came by one day and said, "Hey, let's go to Florida," I dropped the job and headed out for a new adventure. While I was in Florida I met an attractive blonde from Ohio who was traveling the country and working wherever she could. I was instantly smitten with her and she even invited me to leave Orlando soon and travel with her. But as much as I wanted to go, my self-image just wouldn't allow me to believe that an attractive young woman like her could be truly interested in a fat bastard like me, I went back to my parent's home in Topeka and my dad helped me get a job with the state where I worked nights and slept during the day. My depression was still growing though; I was still faltering in school and I felt more lost and desperate than ever, but I never once let go of my intent to go away and to come back a lean, revitalized man.

Finally, I came home one day and my Uncle Pete had returned from his first stint in the Marine Corps. I couldn't believe my eyes when I saw him. He was lean, muscular and very athletic-looking. When we played basketball he could jump higher than I ever saw him jump before and he never seemed to run out of gas, no matter how long or how hard we played. His transformation was truly the stuff I had been intending in my own life, and it wasn't long before I realized I had found my answer. I had decided at age eight or nine that I also wanted to live in California and I spent endless hours lying in that bed, staring out those bedroom windows dreaming about it, so I decided I could kill two birds with one stone and I went to visit my local recruiter.

I left for San Diego that July 31st at age 20, weighing 305 pounds and knowing without question that my intent was guiding my life. When I returned in December 110 pounds less than I had been a few months before,

I was buzzing with the reality of my accomplishment. It was exactly how I had intended it so many years earlier; everyone recognized my voice, but no one recognized my face or my body. I was not shy about asking some attractive woman out and they were not shy about accepting my invitations. My unbending intent had taken me to my fondest dream and I had awakened in the very middle of it.

> *"Strength does not come from physical capacity.*
> *It comes from an indomitable will."*
> *~ Mahatma Gandhi ~*

****

A few months after my trip to Russia I decided to visit some friends down in Lima, Peru. I kind of like Peruvian women anyway, so I am always looking for a good excuse to go there and see the sights. I took the trip soon after the local terrorists had tried to bomb one of the entrances to the U.S. Embassy, which looked like a small fortress. The bombers weren't very successful with the embassy, but they did manage to blow all of the windows out of the new strip mall across the boulevard from the embassy entrance. The windows had all been replaced by the time I arrived and everything looked new and untouched. I had invited the Inorganics to join me at the strip mall, so Friendship and I took a seat in a nice little café and ordered some soup and a salad.

Friendship had taken on the look of a Peruvian professional woman and she looked great. She was wearing a short skirt and had the nicest looking olive-toned legs. We laughed and played with each other and with our server until the rest of the Inorganics arrived. All of the other Inorganics looked Peruvian too, with jet black hair, dark eyes, and olive skin. Self-Importance was wearing a low-cut top and sporting large, full breasts.

Self-Importance: "¡Ay carajo! ¿Vas siempre a llevarme a un restaurante caro?"

("Oh, damn! Aren't you ever going to take me to a nice expensive restaurant?")

Me: "Not with an attitude like that."

138

Self-Importance: (Looking at me coyly) "Hablarme en español, Ricardito, tu sabe que amo que el acentúa americano."
("Speak to me in Spanish, Richey, you know how I love that American accent.")

Me: (Being polite) "Prefiero inglés si no obedece, es mucho más fácil para me."
("I prefer English if you didn't mind because it is much easier for me.")

Self-Importance: (Looking annoyed and switching to English) "Oh damn, you are such a spoil sport."

Romance: "You should humor her, Richard. It might keep her in a better mood while we talk."

Jealousy: "Forget it! His Spanish sucks so let him speak English and we can get on with this."

Friendship: (Looking at me teasingly) "Well, I think your Spanish is cute, so you can use it anytime you are with me. But don't fret if I can't understand your poor pronunciation skills."

That caused some laughter and lightened the mood a bit, so we got down to business.

Me: "Look, I invited you all to meet me here because I am about to write one of the last chapters of my book and I have decided to dedicate it to your points of view."

Monogamy: (Perking up and looking a little surprised) "Really? You will print whatever we have to say and you won't censor it or edit out our most important points?"

Me: "That's correct. I'll give each of you equal space, if you want it."

Monogamy: "No way!"

Jealousy: "Yeah, I don't believe him either."

Me: "Yes, I will. I am serious about this. This is your chance to say exactly what you want to say. I get the last word, of course, because it is my book, but you can say whatever you like and I'll write it all down, within reason, of course."

Monogamy: "See? There is a catch."

Self-Importance: "Since you get to go last, Richey, I want to go first."

Me: "Okay, that's all right with me."

Jealousy: "She always gets to go first. I want to go first just one time."

Self-Importance: "Oh hush, you wouldn't have even thought about it unless I had said something to give you the idea. Besides, people aren't always jealous, married, romantic, monogamous, or divorced, but most people always feel self-important."

Romance: (Chuckling) "Hey, she has a point there. (Looking at me) Have you tried to drive in this city's traffic? Talk about a bunch of people who think they are more important than anyone else on the road!"

Me: (Nodding acknowledgment at Romance) "Okay, here is the deal. I cannot do each of your individual interviews in a group like this, so you'll have to take turns meeting with me individually so we can focus on the questions, answers and statements you want to make."

Divorce: "Hey, why don't you meet me in Hawaii, Richard? I have some honeymooners over there who are ripe for a little wakeup and shakeup."

Me: "Well, we'll see, Divorce, but I am not sure the timing will work, so you'll probably have to meet me somewhere more convenient."

Jealousy: "Oh, yeah, some place convenient and exotic, like Albuquerque."

Me: "I like Albuquerque."

Romance: "Yeah, but does Albuquerque like you? You were sneezing your fool head off over there in November."

Self-Importance: "Yeah, why don't you just intend those nasty old allergies away like you did with all of us? (She leans toward me to let her full Peruvian breasts almost fall out of her low cut top and to imitate being sexy) You know, honey, I've never made you sneeze like that."

The whole group let out some belly laughter, including me.

"Deal with the faults of others as gently as with your own."
~ Chinese Proverb ~

12
Book Twelve:
REVELATIONS OF
THE INORGANICS:

"Great minds discuss ideas;
average minds discuss events;
small minds discuss people."
~ Eleanor Roosevelt ~

I had an appointment in the city of Hermosillo, Senora, which is located in Northern Mexico about 200 miles south of Nogales, Arizona, and I made reservations to stay at the San Sebastian Hotel for a few days. The hotel's restaurant was very nice and featured a sumptuous buffet and very comfortable surroundings for a relaxing meal and conversation, so I encouraged Self-Importance to meet me there. I was always curious about how she would look and I was rarely disappointed with the appearance she selected. She knew my tastes all too well and did her best to make sure I was completely dumbstruck with her physical beauty. I, of course, would always act like I didn't notice, but the moment she entered any room my eyes would immediately find her and my body would buzz with physical attraction and anticipation.

In most restaurants it is my habit to pick a table where I can sit with my back to the wall, see the majority of the inside dining area, and also be able to watch the entrance. In this particular instance I was also able to see the driveway to the front door of the restaurant, so I watched it as I ate to see how Self-Importance would arrive. She loves fanfare and is a total attention junkie, so I knew she wouldn't arrive inconspicuously and then come in and sit down quietly. As I took a bite of a papaya fruit salad I noticed a big, shiny, new black Mercedes Benz with dark-tinted windows roll in to the driveway. It was moving a little too fast and it came to a sudden halt right at the front door. I knew then that my guest had arrived and I couldn't wait to see the fuss that she was about to create. I scanned the room and saw several people who mostly looked like business people watching the car, because this type of blatant affluence in a city like Hermosillo wouldn't go unnoticed. The driver's door swung open and a small, well-dressed man jumped out of his seat and ran around to the rear door on the other side of the car. He grabbed the door handle and stepped out of the way as he held the rear door open. Everyone in the restaurant who could see outside was watching and those who couldn't see were trying to.

After a brief moment of waiting, a black boot with a long spiked heel finally appeared and made its way to the pavement. The boot was followed by a second boot and then two beautifully-shaped, olive-toned legs and thighs emerged with them. Self-Importance's skirt was short and black, hiked up to her crotch, and revealed flawless legs that any human being could easily appreciate. I looked around at the other men in the restaurant who had stopped chewing, dropped their jaws wide open, and sat staring with their mouths full of food. The driver offered his hand and she took it gently as her head and upper torso appeared from the backseat of the car. As she leaned slightly forward to pull herself up and out of her seat her small sequined black jacket stretched open to reveal two large and full round breasts dangling from a small, low-cut white blouse. The white blouse had a large ruffle down the middle to cover its buttons; it was skin tight, had long sleeves with big cuffs and cufflinks past the sleeves of her jacket, and looked as if it would burst open at any moment from the outward pressure of her breasts trying to escape. The black jacket was fastened by one shiny button at the waist, but stretched open widely around her breasts as if to reveal and yet support them at the same time. Her face and eyes were eloquently adorned with just the right touch of makeup and her long, thick, wavy black hair was pulled to one side and hung beautifully down the front of her left shoulder.

Once she was outside of the car, the driver hurried the few steps to the front door of the restaurant to open it for her as well. All the eyes of the diners were still upon her as she stopped in the doorway and turned sideways to face the driver and give him some last-minute instructions. Like all of the other men, I looked her up and down and couldn't help but notice and appreciate the shape and curves of the profile that her tight clothing revealed. Her tight round butt and full protruding breasts were truly the image of physical beauty that otherwise cautious men would sell their souls and good sense to have.

In true self-important fashion she turned and entered the restaurant without looking at the men who lusted so openly for her as she passed by them. Her strut was one of perfection and her breasts bounced invitingly as she headed directly for my table. But just as she was about to reach me and was passing by a table of six very well-dressed businessmen, she bumped ever so slightly into the big leg and foot of one man who immediately jumped up to offer his apologies and strong hands to stabilize her. Two other men at the table also rose immediately to their feet as well and offered apologies for the unforgivable rudeness of their big clumsy friend who had tripped her. I chuckled quietly to myself as I watched the scene and then got up to humor her with my feigned chivalry by offering her a chair.

The men watched her carefully for a while after she took her seat and looked us both over to try to deduce our purpose and relationship.

Self-Importance: "¿Hola, Ricardito, cómo has estado?"
("Hi, Richey, how have you been?")

Me: "Hola, chica bonita, estoy bien, gracias."
("Hi, you cutie, I'm good, thanks.")

Self-Importance: (Complaining as usual) "¿No podrías encontrar un lugarcito bonito?"
("Couldn't you find a little nicer place?")

Me: (Direct and unapologetic) "No, este es el mejor que te pueden ofrecer."
("Nope, this is the best they have to offer.")

Self-Importance: (She picks up a menu and switches to English without me requesting it) "Okay, Richey, baby, I'll be set as soon as I order us a nice taste of wine."

She signals for a male server who has been watching her closely and he almost runs to the table to take her request. She declines food but orders the most expensive wine she can find on the menu. Before the man walks away she stops him and tells him to bring her two extra bottles of the same wine unopened so she can take them with her when she leaves.

Self-Importance: "All right, Richey, darlin', shall we get down to business?" (She reaches up with her right hand and brushes her long hair off her left breast, then turns to smile at the man she just tripped over.) "You may not know it, Richey, honey, but that man is absolutely loaded."

Me: "You don't say?"

Self-Importance: "Oh, yes, I do. He is loaded, single, no kids, and a perfect target for a lovely young señorita like myself."

Me: (Jokingly, but also serious) "Young? You must be tens of thousands of years old by now."

Self-Importance: (Looking back at me) "Oh, don't be such an ass. I am young to him and that's what counts. Besides, he needs some attractive young thing to take care of and to pamper."

Me: "He does look ripe for the pickin', I'll admit."

Self-Importance: (Using her most sexual gaze and voice as she looks back at the man) "Oh my, Richey, darlin', he's just perfect."

The man is watching her closely and he looks back and forth from her to me to catch signals as to what he should or shouldn't do. I just smile and nod at the guy, which confuses him even more.

Me: "So, tell me truthfully, what do you really think of men like him?"

Self-Importance: (She turns back to give me a serious look.) "He's perfect, really! He is exactly the kind of guy a girl like me would want to take home to meet Mommy. He is rich by Mexican standards for sure, he is handsome, educated, owns a nice home and could keep a girl in the style to which she has become accustomed." (She turns to give him another smile.)

Me: "So how long do you think an arrangement like that could last?"

Self-Importance: "Are you kidding? It could last a good many years, just as long as he is willing to keep taking care of me."

Me: "So? Is that what marriage means to you? Finding someone to be your caretaker?"

Self-Importance: "Okay, Richey, look. I'm a Siren for Marriage, among other things, but since we are discussing marriage I'll stay on this topic for now. I create and nurture human Sirens for Marriage because there are so many men out there who enjoy our company, loyalty, and the way we take care of ourselves, so the least they can do is finance it all."

Me: "So you really think it is the man's responsibility to take care of the woman?"

Self-Importance: (As if I'm crazy) "Of course, I do! Just look at me! Do you know how easy it is to find men who will take care of a woman who looks like I do? I get marriage proposals every single day and I can have my pick of any man I want. Besides, it was you men who started this idea of taking care of women anyway."

Me: "Things change, you know?"

Self-Importance: "Not that much, because even the laws you men have made entitle us women to your holdings."

Me: "That doesn't make it right."

Self-Importance: "Sure it does."

Me: "How do you figure?"

Self-Importance: "Well, think about it. Although most men never really consider this fact when they are in love and especially when they are in lust, marriage is a legal contract. When they say 'I do' and sign on the dotted line, the women become their legal partners and in the Western world, they instantly own about sixty-five percent of the man's cash and assets."

Me: "And this sounds right and just to you?"

Self-Importance: "Absolutely! When a woman starts to share her body with a man, she has usually extracted the agreements out of him that she needs to feel comfortable with the arrangement she has made. If they decide to get married and the woman expects to be a homemaker and the man agrees, then he has made a legal marriage contract that obligates him indefinitely to take care of his woman."

Me: "Yeah, but what if they divorce?"

Self-Importance: "So? What if they do?"

Me: "Well, if the woman hasn't worked much, or at all, and they have kids the man usually has to pay heavily to keep her in the lifestyle they maintained when they were married, and usually in the house he paid for too."

Self-Importance: "Such is life. He married her knowing that she expected to him to take care of her, so just because they separate and divorce doesn't mean he is off the hook. He still has a long-term obligation to her and the marriage certificate made it official. If he didn't read the fine print it is his own problem."

Me: "When and where does his obligation end then? And where do his rights as a homeowner and father begin?"

Self-Importance: "His obligation doesn't end, at least until she has found someone else to take care of her, and even then she may still have legal avenues to keep him paying. And as far as the house goes, once he is out he loses all rights to the place. If the ex-wife decides to trash the place it is totally up to her. If she decides to move the pool guy or carpenter into the house and screw his brains out every night, then it is her right and the ex-hubby has to pay the mortgage and other bills regardless. He is legally obligated to do so and this makes it right."

**"If women didn't exist, all the money in the world would have no meaning."
~ Aristotle Onassis ~**

Me: "Men really need to be a lot smarter, don't they?"

Self-Importance: "Maybe. But come on, Richey darlin', if you start trying to cover all of the ends and outs of marriage you'll take all of the romance and fun out of it. Women want to keep their image of a fairytale wedding and fairytale marriage in which they'll always live happily ever after. There are millions of little girls who love to dream of Prince Charming coming to love and support them and they live their entire lives in anticipation of this event. Not all little girls have this dream, of course, but the Sirens of Marriage do and they should be able to keep it."

Me: "I guess there has to be a lot of Prince Charmings out there to make this work, but I still think the guys should be a lot smarter. My buddy gave the house, car, furniture, and several thousands of dollars each month to his ex, but he couldn't even stay in the guestroom of the house he bought and paid for when he went to visit his family because his ex's new boyfriend didn't like it. So it seems to me that guys should wise up and stop signing marriage licenses until it becomes a much more pragmatic process and less emotional and whimsical."

Self-Importance: "My god, you are such a damned spoiled sport! Have a sense of humor, Richey, and let tradition run itself. I don't feel sorry for your buddy at all because he married the woman and took care of her the entire time they were married, right? So he made an agreement, subtle as it may have been, and now he has to honor his end of it and pay up until she no longer wants or needs his financial help to maintain her lifestyle."

Me: "So as far as you are concerned, marriage should remain as it is?"

Self-Importance: "Absolutely! But I would recommend that women be more careful about marrying men who require them to sign prenuptial agreements. The marriage license and saying 'I do' is a contract in and of itself and the courts can enforce the parameters of it when necessary. Women have been very successful in legislating rights and protection for themselves the past few decades, so I think marriage should remain as it is. If men want to get a better deal then they should be as proactive as women have been and they should seek their own legislative protections and remedies, even though you and I both know they won't. But in the meantime, little girls should be able to keep their dreams of Prince Charming and being taken care of in all ways."

Me: "You believe this even though marriage isn't working as it is and the divorce rate is so high and still climbing?"

Self-Importance: "Look, honey, forget all of that practical mumbo jumbo and let me give you the bottom line here. I want to be more important to you than your buddies are, and even more important than your other family members are. This is what marriage and falling in love with someone are all about. Don't you get it? If you change marriage into something else then what's the fun of losing all sense of yourself and giving into that fantastic feeling of being swept away by overwhelming emotional and physical chemistry? People want to fall in love and to forget the legal and practical ramifications of their actions until they are way down the road and it is too late. Humans have learned to establish their own sense of self-worth by how important their significant others make them feel, and this isn't something that is easily changed. And if and when it ends, then it ends, and everyone is free to run off and to do it over and over again until they get enough of it. Who the hell knows how many times we can fall in love and lose all sense of sobriety and pragmatism? So why not go out and find out until you die?"

Me: "Thanks, but I believe I have had as much 'losing myself' as I can handle for one lifetime."

Self-Importance: "Yeah, you big sissy, and you haven't even touched your wine either. What a waste. And to think; you could be married and could wake up to someone who looks like me every day if you would just forget about emotional sobriety and those boring practicalities of friendship."

Me: "Actually, I prefer a woman who is more accommodating and doesn't need to manipulate me by withholding."

Self-Importance: "That's why you gave up on me?"

Me: "It's not that I gave up on you; I just stopped letting myself be manipulated and pushed around by you."

The man that Self-Importance had been flirting with earlier paid his bill and walked outside with his friends, but he didn't leave and was waiting in his car outside in the parking lot. Self-Importance motioned toward the man and took a deep breath before she pressed her point.

Self-Importance: "You see what I mean, Richey, dear? That man is outside waiting on me just in case he gets the chance to say hello again and strike up another conversation. I haven't done anything but flutter my eyelids at him a little and I already own him heart, body, soul, and bank account. By the time I am done with this guy I'll be living in that big house by the country club, driving expensive new cars, wearing beautiful new fashions, and having his cute little babies. (She runs her hands up the front of her lovely body) And it will be him instead of you who is snuggling up with this killer body each night and getting to fuck me, whenever I am in the mood of course." (She flashes me a wily smile.)

"A woman's appetite is twice that of a man's."
~ Sanskrit Proverb ~

Me: "You are so predictable. Okay, how about if we meet up and spend a week together in Barcelona or Madrid soon? I'll even let you pick the hotel and restaurants?"

Self-Importance: "Really? Are you serious?"

Me: "Sure, why not? Uh, with some cost limits of course."

Self-Importance: "Can we go to Paris too?"

Me: "Okay, I suppose we could do that."

Self-Importance jumps up and bends over to hug my neck and press her lovely breasts in my face.

Self-Importance: "Oh, Richey, you can be such a dear at times."

Me: "Yes, I can, but you have to promise to stop calling me 'Richey,' at least in public."

Self-Importance sits back down on the edge of her chair, but faces me and scoots her chair as close as she can. She lay her head on my shoulder and wraps her arm through mine.

Self-Importance: "Okay, I'll stop with the Richey nickname if you let me pick the hotel and restaurants in Paris too."

Me: (Playfully) "Ugh, more blackmail."

Self-Importance: "Yeah, but you love it. Besides, you wouldn't want me to act like I am easy, would you?"

Me: "I love it when you are easy for me, and less expensive too, so we'll apply the same cost limits on Paris."

Self-Importance: "If I become easy for you, will you pay my bills and give me a nice place to live and a nice car to drive with a big allowance?"

Me: "If you were easy for me and completely dependable, I would probably give you a good job and you could take good care of yourself."

Self-Importance: "Hmm? That is an interesting proposition and I'll give it serious consideration."

Me: "It sounds better than always manipulating and coercing some man into taking care of you, doesn't it?"

Self-Importance: (She leans back in her chair and lets out a sigh of resignation.) "There is a lot to be said for a free ride."

Me: "Yeah, but you already know how it always turns out. So what fun is that?"

Self-Importance: "Look, Richey, you know that most people go through life backwards so time hits them from behind. This way they can say things like, 'Oh, I didn't see it coming', and 'I never knew she was cheating on me', and they don't have to take responsibility for anything. You know that ignorance is bliss. But if everyone turned around to face time coming at them, they would have to take full responsibility for all of the outcomes they experienced, and I just cannot see men doing this. I think that men like to be used by me, because why else would they allow it?"

Me: "That's a good question and I admit it will be work for men to see things coming at them, but I also think it is inevitable and part of their evolution."

Self-Importance: "You know why they won't. They'd have to stop thinking with their dicks, and how likely is that?"

Me: "At a certain time in a man's life he usually figures this out and stops doing it. Well, the majority of us figure it out."

Self-Importance: "Oh, yeah? Figuring it out and acting on it are two different things, dear. Do you remember the first time you figured out what I was doing to you? We had been going to Cal State together and you really had the hots for my cute little Greek ass back then."

I instantly remembered a cute little Greek girl I had dated in college and how much I liked her little butt. It was really quite perfect and I should have realized years before now who that had been.

Me: "So that was you." (I said more as a realization than a question.)

Self-Importance: "But of course, Richey, dear, who else could it have been?"

Several years ago I had been dating a young Greek girl I had met in one of my psychology classes. She first attracted my attention because of her luscious little body, but I soon found out that she was also extremely bright. In fact, she fit many of the pictures I had of what is sexy, feminine and attractive, so my interest in her grew more rapidly than I had anticipated. It wasn't long, however, before I realized her need to be pursued far outweighed my energy level and desire to chase, so I declared platonic friendship and broke off my romantic quest. Although she never openly admitted it, it wasn't long before I became aware that my retreat was not at all appreciated. It seemed that we could rarely get together as friends without my feeling the brunt end of her displeasure over something that never really mattered. I liked her a lot, but her controlling nature and frequent feisty responses to me were not really the most pleasant of experiences.

One warm summer morning we were sitting out front of Cinnamon Productions on a bench. We were enjoying our caffeine and chatting about life and relationships when she decided that I had not given the appropriate response to something she had just said. She accused me of being a schmuck and started critiquing my character in less than flattering terms. I had responded to her query with my honest and true feelings, so I couldn't understand why she was verbally assaulting me; and then I started to feel offended. As I sat there listening to the outrageous comments and adjectives she was using to describe me, I started to feel hostility welling up in the midsection of my body. This woman knew me quite well by now and had more than enough information to know that the charges she was making were pure nonsense. The more she went on the more the anger tightened its grip on me and climbed upward toward my chest. While I sat there experiencing the rise of anger I began to have the distinct impression of some foreign manipulation working on me from the outside. Eventually, I somehow managed to detach myself from her words and started to focus my attention on the phenomena that was occurring in my body.

I had the thought that I didn't have to give in to this feeling of anger and that I didn't like the way some foreign force was pulling it up. I was still aware of my friend's presence next to me, and that she was still talking, but I could no longer hear her words, nor did I care about anything she had to say. I could see her on my right from the corner of my eye while she talked and looked at me as if waiting for some response. But I made a decision and told myself no, that I wasn't going to give into the anger that was nearly encompassing my entire body by this point, and then a very abrupt event took place. At the exact moment I made the decision not to give in to the anger welling up in me, I saw this very bizarre-looking cone-shaped energy coming from a small point on the top of my little friend's head. Similar to a whirlwind that appears as a smaller point on the ground, then opens gradually to a much wider cone as it stretches itself upward, this cone made its way up, then turned in my direction and the wide section came down over my head and shoulders to my chest. Then suddenly, at the moment I made the conscious decision to release the anger, it was as if the cone were pulled back by some strong elastic force and it snapped back into my friend's head with such a jolt that it literally made her body jump from the impact. It happened so quickly that it also startled me, but I noticed immediately that my feelings of anger and frustration were instantly gone. I turned to look at her and she had the most surprised and bewildered look on her face, but I decided not to say anything and just let it go.

Me: "What the hell was that, anyway? And how the hell did you do that to me?"

Self-Importance: (Gloating) "You know perfectly well what that was, Richey, honey, don't be such a nincompoop."

Me: "It looked like some sort of energy field you covered me with from the top of your head?"

Self-Importance: "Duh..."

Me: "Can anyone do that?"

Self-Importance: "My god, you can be so exasperating, you know? Of course anyone can do that, and you humans do it to each other all of the time. In English you call it pushing someone's button."

Me: "Yes, in fact, we do."

Self-Importance: "The only difference between you and most people is that you made a decision to let go of the anger and become aware of what was happening to you. The average moron just gives in to the anger and everyone is content. But not youuuu...noooooo...you have to understand and observe everything that happens to you, or that appears to happen to you."

Me: "Well, just be thankful that I do."

Self-Importance: "Why would I do that?"

<u>*Me:* "Because my awareness of you allows me to enjoy you instead of just being constantly annoyed."</u>

Self-Importance abruptly stands up and gathers her little purse along with her two bottles of wine. She smiles deviously at me as she begins to turn and leave.

Self-Importance: "Okay, honey, I don't want to keep that fellow outside waiting much longer, so if we're finished I'll go and introduce myself to him *and to the thinking tool between his legs. He'll buy me anything I want because I am a virtuous woman, but the sooner we get started...* " *(She gives me a look of knowing and turns and walks toward the door.)*

Me: "Let me know if you have anything else to add to your interview before the book goes to print. "

Self-Importance: (She turns her head slightly without looking back at me.) "The only thing I could add is that you are a royal asshole for always letting me go like this. " (She stops and turns back to look at me with another devious smile) "And you're an asshole for taking me to cheap restaurants too. "

I just laugh and wave goodbye to her.

Me: "See you soon. "

Self-Importance: "In Madrid, and I'll make the reservations for us. Oh, and one other thing: You'd better rest up and be prepared for the time of your life, because I'm going to give you anything your little heart desires. "

"Men always want to be a woman's first love.
Women have a more subtle instinct:
What they like is to be a man's last romance. "
~ Oscar Wilde ~

****

A short time later I found myself at a little sidewalk café in the heart of the business district of Victoria, British Columbia on Vancouver Island in Canada. My buddy Samuel and I had driven our van onto the ferry and took it over from Port Angeles, Washington. It was a beautiful day and we had just watched the killer whales swimming all around us on the ferry ride over. I ordered another mocha java while Samuel left me alone to make some business calls. As I sipped my coffee, I couldn't help but notice what a European look the city has, and I was especially taken by how many attractive women I saw. My waitress was a serious cutie and I was just making some headway with her when Jealousy walked up and plopped her big butt down in the chair across from me. My waitress gave me a distrustful look as she came to take Jealousy's order, and then she left us completely alone after Jealousy rudely barked a few commands at her.

As usual, Jealousy looked a bit disheveled and her clothing looked like she had slept in them. I started to ask her why she didn't take better care of herself, but then I realized the question would make no sense to her at all. She probably had no idea how she looked to me and I figured it was better to leave it that way. She rested her large heavy breasts on the table, then raised her elbows and placed them on the table next to her breasts, and laid her chin in her hands.

Me: "My, are we in a lovely mood today?"

Jealousy: "Oh, blow it out your ear, you bastard. You'd be out screwing that waitress tonight if I hadn't come along to interrupt your absorption in her."

Me: "Yeah, so?"

Jealousy: "She's not who you think she is."

Me: "Well, since I didn't even know her name until five minutes ago that could easily be true."

Jealousy: "Trust me, she's not your type."

Me: "Oh, what's my type?"

Jealousy: "A woman who will be happy fucking you the rest of her life without any promises of marriage, and she wouldn't be. She's looking for a husband and not a user like you."

Me: "You know we could always do this interview another time when you are feeling better?"

Jealousy: (She looks at me as if she is surprised by my comment) "Why? I feel fine."

Me: (Not wanting to piss her off any more than she already appeared to be) "Okay, then share your position on coupling with me and why you feel about it the way you do."

Jealousy: "I'm sure you already know how I feel, don't you?"

Me: "I think so, but I need it in your own words, so you can represent your own thoughts and opinions."

Jealousy: "Ha! I buy that, but okay, what exactly would you like to know?"

Me: "I want to know why Inorganics like you are so afraid of the change that people like me want to promote and encourage?"

Jealousy: "Oh, come on, Richard, you know the answer to this already. We have to live, just like you have to live, and we don't want our food supply interrupted any more than you want yours messed with. Besides, Inorganics are not capable of change on their own; it takes you humans to initiate and nurture the change in us."

Me: "Okay, I understand this, but how does changing the traditional practice of relationships and marriage do this, especially to you?"

Jealousy: "To answer you I'll have to share a secret that only a handful of people have ever known."

Me: "Cool, fire away."

Jealousy: "Self-Importance and I were born at nearly the exact same time." (She looks at me and waits for a deeper understanding of something implied.)

Me: "Yeah?"

Jealousy: (Rolling her eyes) "Don't you get it? Self-Importance and I are twins. We entered the world together as a pair, and we operate as a pair."

Me: (Thinking about this revelation) "So if relationships change, you two are separated somehow or are no longer a pair?"

Jealousy: (Looking exasperated) "No! You idiot!" (She stops to think for a moment.) "Okay, let's use your friend Sylvia as an example. How long have you known her now?"

Me: (Genuinely thinking about it.) "Oh, about five or six years, I think."

Jealousy: "All right, you have known her quite a while and long enough to know all too well that Sylvia fell in love with you years ago and wanted you two to be an exclusive couple, right?"

Me: "Uh, okay."

Jealousy: "You also know that every time you would go some place without an explanation, or you would go to see family members without inviting her, or would go out on the weekends without telling her who you were with, etc., that she found this behavior extremely troubling?"

Me: "Well, she's not like that anymore, but I know what you mean."

Jealousy: "If Sylvia had things the way she wanted them, you two would be living together in a committed, monogamous relationship, whether you married or not. And she would feel like she is the most important person in your life."

Me: "Yes, that is true, but she really has learned to be my friend, first and foremost."

Jealousy: "Oh, yeah? And when was the last time you had a phone conversation with her that ended up with her in tears and telling you that you don't give a rat's ass about her feelings?"

Me: "Okay, there was one incident just recently, but it had been a long time since the one before; so what's your point?"

Jealousy: "Sylvia is just like the vast majority of women in your world and society. She wants to be the most important person in your life, and when she realizes she is just an equal to everyone else, what does she do?"

Me: "She has a fit of jealousy, of course."

Jealousy: "Exactly! You see what I mean now?"

Me: "I suppose I do. What you are saying is that <u>if she learns to be my friend and stops competing to be the most important person in my life, then there is no need for her to feel self-important or to have fits of jealousy.</u>"

Jealousy: "And that part of her that feeds me and my twin Self-Importance dies, and we no longer have her as a source of nourishment. But Sylvia doesn't completely realize yet that it's us, me and Self-Importance, instead of her who are actually dying, because she thinks that she is us."

Me: "Well, the dying off of the jealousy part sounds okay to me."

Jealousy: "Of course it does, because you are a selfish bastard and you don't give a damn about anyone but yourself. But don't forget, if it weren't for us it is not likely that you and Sylvia would have ever hooked up in the first place."

Me: "Well, I think it is more accurate to say that I don't really care about feeding you and your relatives, and I don't think you helped Sylvia and I get along at all. In fact, I think you make things worse."

Jealousy: "See? You are an inconsiderate asshole too. It is only because of me and my sister Self-Importance that you are even here on this planet."

Me: (Looking a little startled) "Oh, and how do you figure that?"

Jealousy: "Think about it. Your parents were very passionate lovers when they were teenagers, and if they hadn't made a pact to be the most important people in each other's lives and get married, then you wouldn't have been born, ya bum."

Me: "Okay, that's probably very true, I'll admit it; but it is also because of you two that they ended their marriage too."

Jealousy: "So what? They lasted thirty years together and you and your sister should be grateful to my sister and me for breeding them."

Me: "So you're telling me that I wouldn't be here if it weren't for you and Self-Importance."

Jealousy: "Not in this world and lifetime, that's for sure."

Me: "Okay, I'll have to give this one some thought, but don't hold your breath waiting for much gratitude from me or from my sister. I will acknowledge, however, that you do have a place and purpose in this world like everything else does."

Jealousy: "If I wanted any gratitude I sure as hell wouldn't be talking to you, but I think you are seeing my point. Because if it weren't for Self-Importance there wouldn't be many marriages, at least as we know them. And if it weren't for me those marriages wouldn't hold together, because I am the emotion that makes them so passionate. And without us there is no marriage, no committed relationship, and no world as you know it."

"There is no greater glory than love,
nor any greater punishment than jealousy."
~ Lope de Vega ~

Me: "I see what you mean and it is certainly an interesting thought."

Jealousy: "Remember when I first overwhelmed you? I consumed so much of your energy you could hardly function at all."

Me: "Geesh, how could I forget? I thought you were going to swallow me whole."

Jealousy: "You thought it was just fine to run around and screw anybody who'd let you, but when I turned the tables on you by letting you catch me with another man, you really lost it."

In my early twenties I had been dating a petite little beauty named Betty Jean who was about ten years my senior. She was so cute and young-looking that she would often get carded at restaurants and night clubs when we went out for dinner or drinks, and I had no clue about her true age for more than a year. I had met her and her sister at a nightclub one evening and asked for her number when I walked her to her car. I phoned her soon afterwards and we started seeing each other on a frequent basis.

Betty Jean and I dated for nearly two years, but throughout the duration of our affair we never really talked about commitment or monogamy. I had received a key to her apartment soon after we started going out and I came and went as I liked. I usually spent at least one or two nights a week with her and we often got together for lunch during the week. In those days, I was very hormonally driven and required sex on a very frequent schedule; and Betty Jean, bless her heart, always did whatever was necessary to make herself available. Sometimes on her lunch breaks from work we would head out for some restaurant, but would get detoured to my house for a little roll in the hay. We had a really good time with one another for the most part, but nearly a year into our relationship I was starting to feel restless and bored. And I had been seeing other women randomly throughout the entire time we had been dating.

I deliberately went to Betty Jean's house a few times to tell her I was cutting her loose, but after hanging out and visiting with her for a while, I would eventually leave without doing the dirty deed. Eventually, my lack of interest became evident to her and she started to hit the nightclub scene again with her sister. I didn't think anything of it at first, and even volunteered to babysit with her daughter a few times while they had a girl's night out. But Betty Jean would come home in the wee hours of the mornings and would immediately share stories about some great guy or guys they had always met. And on one occasion, she even volunteered that she had met some guy and had given him her number.

Needless to say, my ego and wild imagination started to get the best of me, and alien insecurities began plaguing my mind. I didn't complain or say anything to her specifically, but I started to become more and more available and started showing up at her home more frequently. The more attentive I became, however, the more she poured on the anecdotal stories about chance meetings and planned encounters with new guys, and she began to reminisce about past lovers who had been in her life. Although I still didn't want to give in or openly admit to the intense feelings of insecurity and jealousy I was now wrestling with on a daily basis, my actions clearly revealed to her that she had me on the run, and I didn't have to say a word. Then finally, after months of fighting off the onslaughts of anxiety, Betty Jean dropped the bomb and revealed to me that she had started to date the guy to whom she had given her phone number. It really didn't matter that I had been seeing and sleeping with other women all along, because now I could only think about the one who was about to get away. And my anxiety grew to mammoth proportions.

Feeling paranoid about being abandoned, I demanded and received more sex and spent more time than ever in bed with Betty Jean. It was as if my insatiable appetite for long bouts of sexual intercourse with her had become the only measuring stick I could find to convince myself that the woman was still mine. Never before had I experienced such emotional pain or upheaval, and never before had I been so challenged to find the inner strength to pull myself together. And then, just when I was truly at my highest vulnerability, I drove up to Betty Jean's apartment and saw her standing out front with her arm around this "other guy."

Jealousy: (Laughing) "You almost shit your pants and crashed your car when you drove up and saw me with my arm around that guy."

Me: (Laughing with her) "Yeah, and the look on that poor guy's face when I got out of my car, walked over and took you by the arm and dragged you off to the house."

Jealousy: (Laughing harder) "The dumb bastard, he didn't know what to do."

Me: "I remember that he started to follow us."

Jealousy: "Yeah, and without even looking back at him you told him to stay the fuck out of it if he knew what was good for him. He couldn't get out of there fast enough." (Jealousy bends over in belly laughter and holds her stomach)

Me: "Well, I really didn't plan to hurt him."

Jealousy: (Still laughing hard) "Yeah, but he didn't know that, and you were a big strong guy in those days. I can only imagine what went through that numbskull's mind."

Me: "Hey, I'm still a big strong guy."

Jealousy: "He did call me later to see if I was okay, but then I didn't hear from him again for weeks."

Me: "Well, I can't say that I was sorry to see him go."

Jealousy: (Finally settling down) "You know I didn't really care about that guy. I just wanted to make you jealous and take charge of the relationship."

Me: "Well, you certainly succeeded. I was a mess, and for a long time."

Jealousy: "I know, it was great. You even had trouble keeping your dick hard for quite a while after that. What a wuss you were. I whooped your ass and fed on you for years."

O, beware, my lord, of jealousy!
It is the green-eyed monster which doth mock the meat it feeds on.
~ William Shakespeare ~

****

I had a long layover at JFK in New York City on my way to Europe, so I decided to find a decent restaurant where I could relax and enjoy some good Italian food. It was an absolutely beautiful September day and I had a long flight ahead, so I wanted to get out and enjoy myself. Although I know it is almost pure poison to my sensitive system, I have always loved a rich Fettuccini Alfredo. It had been months since I had had any so I decided that it was time to enjoy a hearty plate full. I walked all around until someone finally gave me some directions to a place that served American food, but also happened to serve Fettuccini Alfredo.

The place smelled absolutely wonderful as I watched the variety of dishes pass by me on their way to other tables. At first I started to second guess my choice of food because so many of the dishes looked so good, but I decided to stick with my plan. It hadn't occurred to me that company might arrive unexpectedly, but I hadn't been seated for more than a few minutes when Serial-Monogamy walked in and joined me at my table.

It had been a long time since I remembered seeing her take on such an overtly sexual appearance, but I had to just sit there and look at her with awe.

She looked absolutely stunning on this specific occasion and I was truly moved. She had on high heels and skin tight jeans that looked like she had been poured into them, with a thin halter top and no bra. Her hair was brown with blonde streaks, long past her shoulders, and she had on the most exquisite set of dangling diamond earrings with a matching diamond necklace. She looked like money and her thinly covered breasts were perfectly shaped with nipples hard and erect from rubbing against the halter top as she walked.

Me: (With genuine appreciation) "Damn woman, you look good."

Monogamy: "Of course I do. Are you only just now noticing?"

Me: "No, I remember times when I thought you were the hottest thing since barbecue grills."

Monogamy: (Looking down the front of her own body) "You're right, I do look good, huh?"

Me: "Absolutely awesome!"

Monogamy: (Spreading and lowering her hands like a game show hostess to indicate her own body as if it were a prize) "See? Don't you wish you could have some of this?"

Me: "I admit, it is damn tempting, no doubt about it."

Monogamy: "Well, you know the rules and the price, so just promise me that you'll never ever be with anyone but me, and you can have it any time you like."

Me: "You know you fit my pictures and have always tempted me, sweetie, but you also know that is not a promise I can make."

Monogamy: (She leaned back in her chair abruptly and started to pout) "Damn you, why do you have to be such a stubborn bastard? And I wore my hottest outfit just for you, too."

Me: "Yes, you did, and I must admit that you look absolutely delicious, but I thought you were going to meet me in Bucharest?"

Monogamy: (Still pouting) "I don't have an outfit like this in Bucharest, so I wanted to wear it for you here."

Me: "Well, I certainly appreciate the thought, and I am enjoying the eye candy, for sure."

Monogamy: "You know it doesn't have to be just eye candy? You could also touch if you chose to do so."

Me: "Oh, yeah? Well, you have to know that I'd love to."

Monogamy: (She takes both hands and bangs them on the table as if she is about to have a small temper tantrum.) "What is it with you? Billions of men in this world agree to my rules to get what they want from me, even when they don't plan to honor them, and you'd rather go without. I just don't understand you at all! Just tell me you'll agree to be true, even though you really won't, and we can go get a room this instant."

Me: (Seriously thinking over her proposition) "I wish I could, because I am sure it would be as nice an experience as it always has been, but you already know that I won't lie to you. So tell me I don't have to ever make promises like that and that you'll be with me and will love me anyway, and then we can go get a room."

Monogamy: (She folds her arms across her chest and sits back in her chair with her bottom lip sticking out in a classic pouting position.) "Just tell me why you don't like me?"

Me: "I like you fine. In fact, I am crazy 'bout ya, baby, but as you know I have decided not to let myself be held hostage like that."

Monogamy: "You know that woman Sherry you dated fit every picture you've ever had about what a woman should be like, and all you had to do was promise to only be with her to have it all, and you couldn't do it. What a moron, Richard. Don't you feel like a real loser now? That woman would have given you everything."

Me: "No, I don't. I certainly miss her, but we all have to decide at some point what type of world we are going to live in and therefore what type of world we are going to spend our energy supporting. And besides, I can love a woman much more deeply and without reservation if she simply accepts me as I am."

Monogamy: "And what's so horrible about supporting my world and being my food? It's not like I am going to terrorize you and beat you into submission (she smiles deviously), although I've certainly considered it."

Me: (Feigning arousal) "Ooooh, baby!"

Monogamy: "Okay, I'll bite—what do you mean you can love a woman more deeply if she accepts you as you are? Isn't this what she's doing even if she makes you promise to be monogamous with only her?"

Me: "No, it's not. She is making her love and affection conditional and then terminal on a single possibility."

Monogamy: "Yeah, so what?"

Me: "What do you mean 'so what'? Are you going to make me promise not to rob banks or steal cars?"

Monogamy: "That's not the same thing."

Me: "Maybe, but your need to control my behavior for sexual access is a set up for failure. If either one of us finds ourselves with someone else by chance, even if it is an innocent thing or only a one time passing event, we have no choice but to follow through with the threat of abandoning each other, not to mention the hurt feelings of betrayal and the pain of splitting the sheets. Why would I want to set my love affair up for an ending like this?"

Monogamy: "Maybe this is the only way your lover can feel like she trusts you enough to give herself to you and to the relationship completely?"

Me: "This may be true for many, if not most women and men alike, but it is still a hostage situation and a product of the implanted social mind.

Making these kinds of rules only set up the couple for rule breaking and failure. Ask any marriage counselor worth their salt if this isn't so."

Monogamy: "But this is the way it has been for decades. And what woman in her right mind wants her man out running around on her, anyway?"

Me: "Why is that the only other option to agreeing with you? I don't think this means that a person is giving his or her mate a license to go out and sleep with anyone that happens to come along. It just means that a couple is eliminating a primary reason for breaking up or divorcing. The couple can certainly make agreements of safety and respect, but the most important thing is that they act like mature adults and develop their own sense of security from within. Our lovers can help us develop our own feelings of security, but they cannot give it to us."

Monogamy: "So you think you are responsible enough to insure a lover's emotional and physical safety without having to make these types of promises and agreements?"

Me: "You know me as well if not better than anyone, so what do you think?"

Monogamy: (She eyes me over with a playful, mocking look of distrust) "I don't know if I'd trust you with my mom, let alone my sister or girlfriends."

Me: "Hey, come on now."

Bigamy is having one wife too many.
Monogamy is the same.
~ Oscar Wilde ~

Monogamy: (She leans forward and takes on a serious expression) "Okay, all joking aside. You know that I serve several very important functions in society. I help to control the birth rate and therefore the world's population; I help contain and control the spread of sexually transmitted diseases; I help to reduce the amount of jealous rages and murders in the world; I keep the societies honest that still practice arranged marriage; and I help to hold otherwise unstable relationships together throughout the world. And these are just a few of my many benefits among numerous others."

Me: "It's true that I see your value in many ways and that my stance on this issue has cost me dearly at times. I have lost the company of some highly intelligent and intensely beautiful women that I truly adored and wanted with every fiber of my being. But then again, in retrospect, I would have to say that one cannot lose something one never had in the first place."

Monogamy: "But what if you could have had them?"

Me: "As long as they coerced me into promises I didn't want to make I don't think I would have ever really had them. But I could have easily accepted a 'don't ask, don't tell' policy, which would be the adult thing to do."

Monogamy: "Interesting. I know you've dated a number of women over the years who didn't even bring the topic up."

Me: "Exactly! So let's start over and if you don't ask I won't tell, and I'll act as if you are the only woman in my life when I am with you."

Monogamy: "Okay, I can see myself accepting this for a while, but sooner or later I'm going to want to know where you are when you aren't with me."

Me: "Maybe, but by then we'll have a really good thing going and you won't want to give me up."

Monogamy: "I suppose it depends upon the quality of the relationship and if I feel safe, loved, and cared for. But who you really want is Surrender. She is exactly your type."

Me: "I've seen you become Surrender before, several times, in fact."

Monogamy: "Yes, but as you know, when we are combined it is in another dimension, although not far from this one."

Me: "How close to that dimension are we now?"

Monogamy gets up and asks me to follow her, so I do. We walk to the back of the restaurant where we find a small hallway that goes to the kitchen. On each side of the hallway are mirrors so that people coming and going from the kitchen can see around the corners to avoid running into one another. Monogamy points to one of the mirrors, takes my arm and positions me just so:

M.CORTES

Monogamy: "If you look into this mirror you can see your own reflection in the other mirror behind you."

Me: *"Yeah, I can, and then some."*

Monogamy: "You can see your reflection and then a reflection of your reflection and so on."

Me: *"Yes, it looks like my reflections go on and on into infinity."*

Monogamy: "How many reflections can you count before they fade off?"

I started counting the number of reflections I could see. As I counted them they seemed to curve off to the right and I counted at least thirty or more before they completely disappeared.

Me: *"I can count about thirty-three or thirty-four before I lose sight of them. They curve slightly off to the right until they are gone."*

Monogamy: *"Each one of those reflections represents another dimension that is parallel to your own. And in each one of those dimensions things are identical except for miniscule differences, until you go several reflections or dimensions away from your current point of reference, or point of view, and then things change more dramatically. When you change something in your life, especially your intent, you align yourself with one of those other dimensions."*

Me: *"Only my intent?"*

Monogamy: *"Yes, the intent aligns you with it, but to accomplish it your new intent usually has to be accompanied with action: the more dramatic the intent and accompanied action, the further away the reflection you can isolate and then step into."*

Me: *"So every possibility already exists simultaneously in all of those endless reflections?"*

Monogamy: *"Absolutely, every direction you can point to is a different future, and the dimensions of each future are separated like these reflections in the mirror, sort of like the layers of an onion. And in whatever direction you choose, the amount of personal power you have determines the distance you can travel."*

I looked in the mirrors and started thinking of worlds I wanted to live in and silently speculated on how many mirrors away they may be.

Me: *"So how many mirrors away am I now from a best-selling book?"*

Monogamy: *(Laughing at me and pulling me back toward our table)* *"You are actually closer than you might think, but I thought you had something else on your mind."*

Me: (Holding my ground and stopping her from pulling me) "Oh, yes, I wanted to know how far away the dimension was where you and Surrender are combined for me."

Monogamy: "You have a one-track mind when it comes to that book of yours."

Me: "What can I say? It really matters."

Monogamy: "Yeah, yeah, yeah."

Me: (Looking back in the mirror) "Okay, show me. How many mirrors away from here are you and Surrender?"

Monogamy: (Looking in the mirror too) "Hmm? I think thirty reflections should do it."

Me: "So only thirty mirrors away and you and Surrender are combined?"

Monogamy: "Well, for you we are, but in this dimension we're combined for other men; men who give us what we want. In the dimension or reality you want, we don't make you give us promises that you don't want to make."

Me: "Hmm?"

Monogamy: "Want to try to step into that mirror?"

Me: "Really? Are you serious?"

Monogamy: (Giggling) "Sure, why not? A leap that far takes quite a bit of personal power for the average guy, but you certainly have enough for a small leap."

Me: "So what do I do?"

Monogamy: "Count thirty mirror reflections away, or just pick one of the last reflections you can see, and then focus all of your attention on that reflection. And when you start to feel yourself being pulled into it, just let go."

Me: "Really, it's that simple?"

Monogamy: "Well, it certainly could be, but <u>most people cling very tightly to what they know and believe</u>. As you are aware, <u>people's expectations and beliefs keep them anchored right where they are.</u>"

Me: "So, you're going to be on the other side of that mirror when I get there? You combined with Surrender, that is?"

Monogamy: "Yup, I'll be there. And you can have anything your little heart desires when you arrive."

I looked in the mirror, counted to the last reflection I could see, and started focusing all of my attention on it. I heard Monogamy whispering something in my ear and then she started to lick and gently bite my earlobe. It was difficult to focus on the reflection with her distracting me, but she finally stopped and I did my best to stop my thinking process and let myself be pulled. After a few moments, I started to feel something tugging at me and I let myself go with it. I felt something like a pop in my head, or in my ears, I wasn't sure, but I lost my focus and felt Monogamy beside me again and she was pressing her lovely breasts into my arm.

Monogamy: "There you are. Welcome back."

Me: (I gave her a surprised look) "What do you mean? I never left."

Monogamy: (She looked surprised) "Yes, you did."

I looked Monogamy over and realized that something looked slightly different, but I wasn't sure what it was. She took me by the arm and started walking us back to our table. When we turned the corner there were three women sitting at the table we had left only moments before, or maybe it wasn't our table and it was only pushed closer to where our table had been. I hesitated and looked at them. Monogamy released my arm and sat down at the table next to the three women. I looked down at the table and it was set almost exactly as we had left it, or had left the table next to us; I was confused. Monogamy slid into her chair, she folded her hands, rested them on the table in front of her, and smiled at me. I decided to go ahead and sit down.

Monogamy: "Do you remember the first time you really recognized me?"

I took my seat and looked at her with confusion all over my face.

Monogamy: "Come on, silly, I know you remember."

I really didn't have a clue what she was talking about and was still taken aback by our sudden change of tables. There was no way we had been gone long enough for those three women to take our seats, order their food, and be served. I turned to look at them and it was obvious that they were nearly finished with their meal.

Monogamy: "Come on, I'll give you a hint. We were in Long Beach on Second Street, in Belmont Shore, and it was a warm Southern California night."

Me: (I shook my head at her) "You'll have to give me more to go on."

Monogamy: "We were in Panama Joe's and you were with two of your buddies, watching a playoff game. I kept watching you and the game as I inched closer, and then to get your attention I did this."

I started feeling a slight tickling sensation in my groin and on the bottom of my testicles. I looked at Monogamy to see how she was doing that when a vivid memory exploded into my head.

I had been with my buddies Jake, who was a big Yankee fan, and Samuel at Panama Joe's in Belmont Shore to watch the Yankees in an American League playoff game. The game was about over and the Yankees were solidly in control, so people were starting to leave the bar. I was standing by a low, narrow room divider that also served as a counter for people to sit their drinks on, and I was watching a television hanging from the wall above the long bar. To my left I had noticed two women who had been seated earlier, but who were now standing only a few feet away. They both looked like professional women and were very well-groomed. One was blonde with shoulder-length hair and she was a few inches shorter than her brunette friend who was relatively attractive. The brunette had shorter hair, only about midway down her neck, and her jeans and thin sweater top were tight, revealing a slightly rounded middle section and large lovely breasts. I noticed the brunette watching me from the corner of my eye as I nursed my beer and then I overheard her girlfriend excusing herself to go to the lady's room. My body was slightly facing the brunette as I turned my head to the right to watch the game.

As I watched the game wind down I saw the brunette stepping sideways to get closer to me. I looked straight ahead so I could see her clearly, but I didn't look directly at her. I watched the scene in front of me and it began to take on an almost surreal kind of quality, sort of like a dream. I am not sure I can explain it, but the light took on a slight haze and it reminded of me of the special effects lights I have seen in some supernatural movies. Then, suddenly, I saw this whip-like tentacle unfurl itself from the middle of the brunette's lower abdomen and slide toward me just above the floor to my feet, where it suddenly turned upward and stopped when the tip touched my testicles. I felt the same tickling sensation then that I was feeling now at the table with Monogamy.

I had a surprised look on my face, I'm sure, as I looked at Monogamy for an explanation. She smiled broadly at me when she realized I was referring to the memory she had just been soliciting.

Me: "But how can that be?"

Monogamy: "How can what be?"

Me: "That wasn't you, that was Surrender. I even talked to her."

Monogamy: "Yes, it was Surrender, and that was me."

Monogamy suddenly transformed herself in front of my eyes and I saw the brunette from Panama Joe's sitting in front of me.

Monogamy: "I know you're not picky, Richard, but you have always had a thing for brunettes, so I just wanted to give you what you like."

I suddenly realized that I had actually made the transition through to the thirtieth mirror I had been focusing my attention on earlier. I suspected it before because of the slight differences I had noticed, but now I knew it for sure. The Monogamy I was now sitting in front of was also Surrender, and she was willing and delighted to give me the things I liked. And all she asked from me in return was that I be kind and give her the respect and love that she deserved.

Me: "Can everyone do that—send tentacle-type feelers across several feet to touch someone?"

Monogamy: "Of course they can, silly, and they do, all of the time. People don't really notice it because they have been socialized not to see such things. And as you well know, that takes a different type of attention. That's all."

Me: "I just remember how surprised I was to see and experience someone do that on a physical level."

Monogamy: (Laughing) "You were so stunned you could hardly talk to me, and I was going to take you home too."

Me: (Chuckling at the memory) "After you left I realized I had passed up a golden opportunity, but the sight and sensation of you tickling my balls from a distance just caused me to freeze up."

Monogamy: "You couldn't even ask me for my number."

Me: "So what else can you do?"

Monogamy: "Come on, Richard, let's go and get a room, and I'll show you a range of other things I can do."

"Your lost friends are not dead,
but gone before,
advanced a stage or two upon that road which you must travel
in the steps they trod."
~ Aristophanes ~

****

I had to go to Las Vegas to meet a friend of mine from Africa who was there to visit some family members. So it was a good excuse to drive over from Los Angeles in my classic black 1982 Jaguar XJ6 with wire wheels and a tan leather interior. I have had the car for many years and it belonged to my buddy Samuel before me, so I know its history and that we have both kept it in mint condition.

Since I was in the marriage capital of the western U.S. and probably the world, I decided to invite Marriage to meet me at the Bellagio Hotel and Casino. Like most Las Vegas casinos, it has a killer buffet, and this one has huge windows so the diners can watch the passing throngs of tourists meander by the dancing water fountains outside. When I arrived I asked the host for a window table, but Marriage already had commandeered a perfect window table that allowed a great view of the diners inside the restaurant and of the outside passersby a floor below. I immediately noticed as I greeted her that she was in her usual aloof and consultative mood, but then I got the impression that after more than ten thousand years of life that this was probably her good mood too. She was wearing a woman's business suit with a white shirt and wide band collar.

Me: "Hey, Marriage, you look like a minister."

Marriage (Very matter-of-fact) "That's because I am a minister."

Me: "You are? I never knew that."

Marriage: "Absolutely. It is one of my more important functions and occupations in this world."

Me: "Really? Why is that?"

Marriage: "Because so many people view me as 'sacred' and this is an image I wish to keep."

Me: "Interesting. Care to elaborate more about this and how it helps you?"

Marriage: (Shifting in her seat as if she means to get right down to business) "Well, as you are aware I was born as a business transaction more than ten thousand years ago."

Me: (Genuinely impressed) "Yes, I am, and that is some life-span you've had. I can't imagine what it must have been like to have walked the Earth all of those years and to have witnessed all of the history you've witnessed."

Marriage: "It's true that I am considered to be ancient, but the time has gone by much faster than you can imagine. You know yourself; the older you get the faster time seems to pass by, and I can assure you that to me a year zooms by and is gone in a flash. In fact, a year goes by for me about as fast as a day does for you. If you really think about it in different terms, however, I am not really all that old."

Me: "How do you mean?"

Marriage: (She raises her eyebrows as she looks me over to see if I am really interested) "Okay, consider this: if you take men who have each lived to be one hundred years old and lay them back to back, meaning that one is born the day that one dies and so on, you would only have one hundred of them from the time of my birth to the present day, and only twenty of them from the time of Christ to the present day."

Me: "Wow, that doesn't really seem like such a huge amount of time when I think of it like that."

Marriage: "So although I am certainly a seasoned veteran, I don't feel as old as one might expect. In comparison to the life-span of most Inorganics, I am a relatively young individual."

Me: (I sit back in my chair to ponder this revelation) "That's truly an amazing concept."

Marriage: "Then, if you compare my life-span to that of the four-billion-year-old Earth or the thirteen-billon-year-old universe, my existence has been little more than the blink of an eye. So is there any doubt about why I wish to continue on as I am?"

Me: "So did you have a lot of growing up pains like we humans do?"

Marriage: "I suppose you could say that. If you count my fetal years I am actually much older than you realize. Up until the time of marriage people tended to couple up for about four years until their offspring could keep up with their mothers, and then they found new mates, It's all in Helen Fisher's book The Anatomy of Love *and Mary Batten's book* Sexual Strategies, *so anyone can read about my pre-infancy years there."*

Me: "How did all these years of life lead you to becoming a minister?"

Marriage: (Looking more serious) "Survival, of course!"

Me: "Survival?"

Marriage: "Sure, survival and power. What's so hard to believe about that? I want to survive just like anybody else and have power in the world."

Me: "And being a minister helps you survive and have power?"

Marriage: "Absolutely! As I was saying earlier, before you focused on my age, I am a clergywoman, monk, medicine woman, and shaman in nearly all religions and spiritual belief systems throughout the globe. And this has served to give me a very long and prosperous existence in this world."

Me: "Can you explain this strategy in a lot more detail?"

Marriage: (She scrutinizes me with her eyes again) "Are you going to let me finish my thoughts if I continue in this direction?"

Me: (Looking guilty) "Yes, yes, I promise. Please forgive me and continue on because I am genuinely interested in this topic."

Marriage: (She takes a deep breath and thinks about her next explanation) "Even though I was born as a business transaction and have remained one for the most part, my infancy and adolescence was rattled with haggling, trading, kidnapping and a lot of chaos in general. Even to this day there have been tribes in the world that will raid other tribes to steal women for wives. So in an effort to bring order to chaos, the spiritual and religious leaders in all corners of the world began to declare marriage as a sacred union. Although it may have been a perfectly acceptable and even necessary social practice to the Yanomamo people in South America to steal their neighbor's women for wives, the more modern societies that were developing the rule of law couldn't tolerate such behavior. It caused too many conflicts and wars between neighbors, countries and even relatives like brothers, uncles and cousins. So by making it a religious and spiritual merger, it became highly regarded as an act of divinely inspired unionization, and people were socially coerced into respecting it and the rights of others to have it."

Me: "Fascinating. So being associated with God and sacredness gave you a new type of protection and ongoing fuel for life?"

Marriage: "Exactly! And as long as people continue to associate me with God, religion and sacredness they will continue to pay me divine homage and are much less likely to question the dictates and policies I set forth in their lives. In the world of love and romance it is physical chemistry that most often brings the couple together and then I take over from there."

Me: "That's a hugely powerful position to be in."

Marriage: "Of course it is, and this is why your buddy Samuel calls me 'the marriage god', because he is acutely aware of my universal power and influence."

Me: "I think I can see why you wouldn't want to give up that kind of power."

Marriage: "Just look at the average couple. I can either destroy their lives with separation and fighting or have them celebrated and honored at anniversaries. And my rule is nearly universal throughout the world."

Me: "I guess you wouldn't be too eager for people to see you as you really are?"

Marriage: "That's exactly right. If people see me as the manmade entity that I really am and that it was only the strategic machinations of humans that made me godlike and sacred, it could change everything forever. What motivation would people have to keep holding me in such high esteem and to keep following my mandates so blindly? Relationship bonding and families would become completely chaotic without me to guide them."

Me: "So you believe that such a discovery would be detrimental to the majority of societies at large?"

Marriage: "Absolutely! Mankind is not yet ready for such revelations. Because aside from the fact that I most certainly want to survive, what would people do in my absence? You know full well as a behavior modification specialist that people need replacement behaviors before most of them can give up common activities, such as overeating, smoking, etc., and what would there be to replace me?"

Me: "You already know my answer to that."

Marriage: "I suppose I do, and although I admit I am beginning to like the idea, I have serious concerns that marriage can grow out of relationships that are built primarily on friendship. Women do it now with much more frequency than men, but the current human mentality requires infatuation, lust and chemistry to bring a couple together. It will be very difficult to build marriage on the foundations of friendship and replace the sacred business deal and the concept of property ownership that now permeates the human consciousness."

Me: "That may be true, but with the high rate of marriages ending in divorce and the rate of divorce still growing, it seems prudent to focus our energies on other alternatives."

Marriage: "I admit that it is highly unlikely you humans will ever be able to maintain the emotional state of infatuation and the state of being in love for decades at a time, although people do keep trying."

Me: "Yes, and the length of success is getting shorter instead of longer."

Marriage: "But doesn't it give you a really good feeling when you meet a couple who has been happily married for thirty, forty, or fifty years?"

Me: "Sure, there is indeed a sense of satisfaction in finding those couples who can do something most of us cannot, but what would they say is the secret to their success?"

Marriage: (Smiling and chuckling) "Probably the fact that they are very good friends, first and foremost."

Me: "I think it is terribly detrimental to children for adults to continue to model bickering and fighting as acceptable marital relations."

Marriage: "That may be so, but it really isn't my concern. Survival is my primary motive."

Me: "Maybe you are still an adolescent that hasn't quite grown up just yet, even though you are so old."

Marriage: (She looks at me with surprised expression) "How do you figure?"

Me: "You said it yourself that you evolved from a brief coupling Inorganic to the omnipresent being you are today."

Marriage: "So?"

Me: "Well, maybe maturity and adulthood for you is further evolution to a world where people form marriage bonds that are based solely on the principles of friendship. Married couples spend so much time fighting and bickering like children that it seems only logical to me that someone needs to grow up. It takes a mature couple to form any type of bond, either long-term or short-term, for the purpose of marriage or child rearing."

Marriage: "So forming bonds that fit a couple's needs instead of them conforming to the norm? Hmm..."

Me: "Well, wasn't it we humans who created marriage?"

Marriage: "Yes, you gave me life."

Me: "Then why can't we tweak it and rearrange it any ol' way we like?"

Marriage: "I think people might assume that this means a life without passion."

Me: "Then they'd be completely wrong, because I already live this way and the passion is more available than ever."

Marriage: "I'll admit that the one thing I know about life here on Earth is that there are worlds layered upon worlds, and any one of them is possible to achieve. So I've little doubt that many of you humans will eventually discover that part of me that exists in other realms. Although I am loath to say it, there are worlds where I exist on the culmination of friendship principles as you have described them."

"For in the resurrection they neither marry nor are given in marriage, but are like angels in heaven."
~ Jesus: Matthew 22:30 ~

****

I checked into the Xinqiao Hotel, which is located about three quarters of mile north of Tiananmen Square in Beijing. Right across the street is a subway entrance to a system that goes just about anyplace in the city and there are great restaurants and shopping areas in close walking distance all around the hotel. Taxis are so cheap in Beijing that the subway is really only necessary as a backup when no cabs are around, which is unusual.

Beijing is a huge and bustling metropolitan city that has new construction going on all over the place. Like Hong Kong, it reminds me a bit of New York City because of all the high rises and millions of people all trying to crowd into small places at once, but no matter what its faults, it is always a treat to be there. The Chinese women in Beijing appear to take very good care of themselves too, and they are beautiful, impeccably dressed creatures by any standard. It is amazing to discover how many of them speak a little English and how friendly they are to westerners. And since I planned to be there for more than a week I decided it would be a good place to let Divorce stop by for our discussion and his individual interview.

We met outside of my hotel by the subway entrance and Divorce said he wanted to treat me to a good restaurant that was in easy walking distance. I decided to follow his lead and we ended up at a Kenny Roger's Roaster that was about five doors away from the McDonalds, two doors away from the Pizza Hut, and catty-corner to the Kentucky Fried Chicken. As we entered the Kenny Roger's restaurant I could smell the spicy aroma of the traditional Chinese seasonings in the American-style stews and casseroles that I knew I wouldn't smell in the same U.S. restaurants. The place was busy, so we had to take the only table we could find, which was one floor below and without any view at all.

Divorce: *"I know you've been in China for a couple of weeks already, so I figured you were due for some good ol' down-home cooking."*

Me: (I don't like the traditional spice I could smell and it doesn't like me either) "That's very thoughtful of you, Divorce, and I appreciate your good intentions."

Divorce: *(He looked genuinely pleased with himself) "No problem, Richard, I'm glad you are happy with the selection I've made for us."*

Me: "So how do you like Beijing?"

Divorce: "Huh? Oh, I like it okay. The people here are still a lot more traditional than they are in the Western world, so the divorce rate is not quite as high as it could be, but it's coming along nicely."

Me: "Well, I'm glad to find you happy with your progress. There is nothing more boring and depressing than someone who is unhappy with their work."

Divorce: (He looks at me carefully to see if I am being facetious) "That's true, and I do enjoy my work, thanks to you humans."

Me: "Apparently you do, because you are highly successful in the U.S. and most of the Western world in general."

Divorce: (Smilingly broadly) "Yes, I am, if I do say so myself."

Me: "So what would you attribute the bulk of your success to?"

Divorce: "Actually, I can attribute it to a number of factors, aside from the help of my fellow Inorganics like Self-Importance and Jealousy, who are extremely beneficial to my efforts and who make my life a genuine pleasure."

Me: "Can you list them for me?"

Divorce: "I guess I would begin with some factors that you are already aware of, such as chemistry."

Me: "Chemistry? How in the world does chemistry help you?"

Divorce: "It helps me because so many people look for it and make it a priority when they are seeking a mate. But chemistry is very transitory and if the marriage is consummated primarily on this factor, which many of them are, I get the couple soon after its effects wear off."

Me: "I see."

Divorce: "Another big issue is one that Marriage mentioned to you earlier about the extended life-spans that humans are now experiencing. For thousands of years you humans have had very short lifetimes and therefore very short marriages, but now that the average life-span of people is approaching more than eighty years, it is damn near impossible for you idiots to get married once and stay married from thirty to seventy years. I mean, my god, who wants to wake up to the same old mug each morning for fifty-plus years?" (He chuckles.)

Me: "Okay, you've got me there."

Divorce: "Imagine someone making a lifetime decision at age 5. I mean, how reasonable would it be to expect a person to keep that decision at age 15 or 20? And if someone makes a lifetime decision at age 15, how reasonable would it be expect this person to keep this decision at age 25 or 30? You humans often change goals and ambitions dramatically from age 25 to 40 and from 40 to 80, so enduring marriage these days is in serious trouble from the beginning."

Me: "I guess the people who would find this length of marriage attractive would be the diehard romantics who still believe in 'happily ever after' and who don't want to give up this dream."

Divorce: "Yeah, have you seen that jewelry store commercial on TV where the old couple is shuffling along, hand in hand, as the young couple walks by them? The younger woman turns to look back at the older couple as she takes her man's hand so we can all see the big fat diamond ring on her finger. The message is this: 'The key to longevity and to staying happily married for a gazillion years is to buy a woman an expensive diamond to prove your romantic love for her'. Ha! What a joke that is. Yeah, go ahead and buy her a ring and then see what she does with it after she divorces your sorry ass and takes all of the rest of your assets too."

Me: "My, my, are we a little cynical today?"

Divorce: (Chuckling and brushing off my comment) "Not at all. I am just a realist and I'm all too aware of how fragile relationships can be when they are built on fleeting romantic notions instead of solid practical planning. It's just like Self-Importance told you in your interview with her, that marriage is a serious business and a legal contract that has numerous ramifications, which most people never fully consider when they are caught up in their romantic fantasies and physical lusts. Young girls dream of being the princess who is rescued by the Prince Charming and young boys dream of being Prince Charming who rescue the princess. But these childhood fantasies rarely ever pan out in the working world of reality, and adults keep pushing the fantasy on the kids anyway, without giving them a clue about the real-life difficulties and consequences of such fantasies."

Me: "Why don't these fantasies translate well into the world of adults?"

Divorce: "Because of self-importance, self-doubts, jealousies, betrayals, revenge, the short shelf life of chemistry, and a host of other emotional crap that people carry with them from childhood. Plus the fact that people just aren't accustomed to multiple decades of being with only one other person. Males really have to fight against strong, influential instincts in order to be with only one person for any length of time anyway. Because of hundreds of thousands of years of evolution, males are instinctually driven to be with a variety of partners, and women just hate this about them. They are not often very forgiving about this either."

Me: "Do you think that marriage and relationships in general would last a lot longer if women were more understanding about men and how we are made?"

Divorce: "Without doubt, because women would realize they are trying to hold men accountable to instinctual drives that are not natural to them, but are natural instead to themselves as females."

Me: "What do you mean?"

Divorce: "It's simple if people are able to set aside the social mind and religious dogma for a moment to consider how they've evolved. We Inorganics were there and we watched and participated in your evolution firsthand. For eons females had to find a strong male with resources who could protect her and her offspring if she wanted to survive. But males, on the other hand, had to get with as many females as possible if they wanted to procreate successfully and make sure their seed survived behind them in the world. And after thousands of years of evolution these have become powerful, instinctual drives that cannot simply be switched off. The unconscious is a powerful driving force, as you humans well know, so it is foolish to think that women can make their men shut down these instincts and not act on them for the next ten to fifty years or so. Women often want to believe their nooky is so good that any man should be happy with it forever, and that because of a religious ceremony or other promises of fidelity that men should only be interested in them."

Me: "Some men can do it."

Divorce: "Sure they can, but you realize that they are far and few between and many of them suffer from severe emotional distress and dependency issues. One only need look at the statistics to see how many married or otherwise attached men fool around. And in this regard, what you have is a bunch of philandering men who have agreed to build and support a system of lifetime bonding that is highly matriarchal in nature, but who in turn are really hypocrites because they say and agree to one thing and do something else entirely. Until some kind of balance occurs, which doesn't appear to be coming real soon, I will have an extremely successful career among you idiots who keep trying to live a life you are not cut out to maintain, at least not for fifty-plus years anyway."

Me: "What about the statistics that say married men live longer than single men?"

Divorce: "I don't know for certain because that's not really my department. But I would bet that there are numerous reasons for this."

Me: "Such as?"

Divorce: "For one, married men tend not to take as many physical risks as single men do, so I'd bet this is a very good reason. For another, married men tend to be more stable in their careers and don't move from job to job and to self-employment as often as single men do, so they keep better health care benefits and for longer periods of time. So I'd bet these two reasons alone would play a big part in that statistical data."

Me: "Okay, that makes sense to me, but it still doesn't change the fact that men and women often have such different drives and expectations in relationships. So what would you recommend if you wanted to change this pattern?"

Divorce: "Ha! You're too funny, like it would be in my best interest to give advice on how to neutralize breakups?"

Me: "Oh, come on. You are wildly successful these days, so how could it hurt to give a little advice?"

Divorce: "Well, if I thought anyone would take my advice on this topic seriously I wouldn't give it, but people are so hardheaded and set in their ways that it is highly unlikely they'd listen to any positive relationship advice I'd have to give anyway."

Me: "Okay, out with it."

Divorce: "First of all, have you ever noticed how often people say 'we're just friends'? When you ask a woman if she is seeing a guy and she isn't dating him she always responds with 'No, we're just friends'. And what this tells you immediately is that she holds friendship in less esteem than she holds lovers or boyfriends, because you never hear them say, 'No, that's just my boyfriend', or 'No, that's just my lover'. Men do it too, so both genders tend to hold friends as less valuable than lovers."

Me: "Yeah, you're right. I hear people say 'just friends' all of the time, and I have even said it too."

Divorce: "If people really wanted to make their relationships work this would be a significant place to start, because let's face it, girlfriends, boyfriends, and lovers in general all come and go in this world. But it is our friends who are still around when these people fade away and it is our friends that we rely upon to help us pick up the pieces when we are devastated by disappointment and failure."

Me: "That's so true."

Divorce: "And you said it yourself that we hold our lovers to different and more unrealistic standards than we hold our friends to. So lovers rarely meet these expectations and come and go, but it is our friends who stay."

Me: "My friends are the best. They seem to stick by me no matter what."

Divorce: "Another thing singles need to be aware of is the potential lover who refers to her split with an ex-spouse as 'my divorce'."

Me: "How's that?"

Divorce: "Because people who refer to the end of their marriage as 'my divorce' are still not finished with it. They still own it and carry it around with them and that's why they refer to it as 'mine'. A person who says, 'I am divorced', has come to terms with it and has accepted it, and a person who says, 'I was divorced', is finished with it, and has moved on."

Me: "So if they are not finished with it they carry it into their next relationship?"

Divorce: "You bet they do and then they bring me their new spouse."

Me: "So what would you do?"

Divorce: "Hey, I like things the way they are, but if it were me, I would start looking for a few good friends that I could convert into lovers, so I'd have a head start right off the bat. And I would place less importance on the initial charge of chemistry everyone is looking to find as well. Most people don't realize it, but chemistry can be built with the right friend. When people build their relationships on that initial buzz of chemistry they discover later that they didn't really put much energy into the practical aspects of friendship, so when the conflicts begin and the chemistry fades, they discover they are sleeping with someone who is actually a stranger, and sometimes a very unpleasant one. But the problem with you humans is that as soon as you have sex with someone you stop treating them like friends and you up the standards for them to live by. So even if you did sleep with your friends, you'd screw it up anyway."

Me: "Yeah, it's an interesting problem, huh?"

Divorce: "You tell me."

Me: "Tell you what?"

Divorce: "About your success?"

Me: "What success?"

Divorce: "Come on, don't play dumb with me. How long did it take you to learn to treat a lover like you would your closest friends, and not change the rules for her?"

Me: "Oh, that. Let's see, I don't know, a lifetime probably. But the difficulty is getting a lover to respond in kind, because just as soon as we get naked, her expectations change and it is no longer okay for me to just come and go as I like."

Divorce: (Shakes his head in agreement) "Yup, the social mind is truly an awesome and powerful force to be dealt with, (He looks at me devilishly) Unless you can find a woman or two who have already traversed this ground too, you are probably in for a very long wait."

Me: "I'm afraid you may be right. The social mind causes people to automatically change their expectations of a significant other they sleep with. But I also think that this is why so many people are choosing to stay single."

Divorce: "Many guys who have been single for a while really don't like it much when women encroach on their territory and put pressure on them to be more available. And the same is true for some women too."

"Women upset everything.
When you let them into your life,
you find that the woman is driving at one thing
and you're driving at another.
~ George Bernard Shaw ~

192

Me: "It's true. And the older men and women get, the less likely they are to want to give up their autonomy."

Divorce: "The bottom line is that people will have to think outside the box and change their values to make friendship the more important and valuable asset over having a lover in the more traditional sense. But I wouldn't take this advice too seriously because it is unlikely that other Inorganics like Self-Importance and Jealousy will ever allow this to happen. And I am personally dependent upon them for this service anyway."

Me: "I know you're thriving and really like things the way they are, but why not expand yourself to more simple forms of breakups, and then you wouldn't be so dependent upon married people for your sustenance?"

Divorce: "You are funny, you know it? Forget it, Richard, I am what I am, just like you are what you are. Asking me to change my modus-operandi is like asking you to stop being a guy, because it ain't gonna happen. And you know better than that anyway. Jealousy already told you that we Inorganics don't have the power to change our own natures and that only you humans can do that."

Me: "Well, it was just a thought."

Divorce: "Look, I like all of the fighting and conflict that goes on in most divorces. No, the bickering and battles are not absolutely necessary for sure, but they are certainly helpful, and the feuding helps to keep the divorce numbers high and climbing. So why would I want this to stop?"

Me: "I suppose you wouldn't."

Divorce: "No friggin' way, man, and the rougher, more volatile and vicious the parents make the split up the more likely the kids will turn out to be just like them. You know it's not the divorce that causes harm to children, it is the fighting between the parents that really causes the pattern to continue, so I'm all for it. It's just like you said, people rear cattle for food, and we rear you for food; it is just the way of things, so why mess with it? I have a great racket going on in this world and the nastier people are to one another the more I like them. As long as men and women have unrealistic expectations of one another that are based upon ancient beliefs of religious partnering that have absolutely no relevance in the modern world, I will thrive. And could you or anyone else blame me? I have a life like anyone else, and I want to survive, no matter what it takes or how many people I have to devour to make it happen."

"The thing that destroys a person is not the knowing,
but the knowing and not doing."
~ Carolyn M. Rodgers ~

I was running out of time and had to get this book to my publisher quickly, so I decided to ask Romance and Friendship if I could do their interview together. It seemed the appropriate thing to do anyway after I had some time to think about it, because I wanted to see how these two would get along and match up as a pair. I really knew the answer to this already, but I have never interviewed just the two of them in an intimate setting, so I decided what the hell. I had a meeting with a very special friend in the Phoenix area with whom I love to hang out, so I decided that this would be the perfect place to meet with Romance and Friendship together.

Although it was an early part of spring it was a hot day in the desert and I cruised over to the Tonto Bar and Grill in Cave Creek, Arizona, in my XJ6. I like hot days in spring because they are a harbinger of the summer months to follow and I do love the summer. In fact, it would be okay with me if I never had to experience cold weather again.

The Tonto Bar and Grill is located on the edge of a beautiful country club golf course, so this symbolic game of summer raised my spirits even higher. I parked the Jag in the shade and out of harm's way, then strolled into the beautifully chiseled Southwest adobe building and found Friendship and Romance inside waiting on me. They both jumped up to give me a hug as I approached the table and Friendship was looking tasty as ever. She was showing her age just a little as she always does, but she wears it in a mature and classy style that only a man of good taste like me could truly appreciate. She rarely attempts to do sexy for me, but it is impossible to ignore the profound and dynamic female energy she emanates and the lovely female figure she maintains.

Romance looked tall, dark and handsome as he always does, but he also looked younger than usual, so I was of course curious about this development. He pulled my chair out for me, then sat down in his own with a huge grin on his face.

Me: "So, Romance, what's up with the totally youthful appearance?"

Romance: (With a big smile) "Oh, so you noticed, eh?"

Me: "Of course I noticed, you look one hundred years younger."

Romance: (He looks at Friendship) "Should I tell him?"

Friendship: (Unabashedly) "Why of course you should tell him. That's one of the reasons we are here."

Romance: "Okay, here is the news." (He pauses.)

Me: "Well?" (I'm smiling impatiently.)

Romance: (Laughing at my eagerness) "Friendship and I have talked it over and we have decided that there is enough human energy available for us to join forces and become mates."

Me: "WHAT! To become mates? Like, as in married?"

Friendship: (Also laughing) "Now don't go and get all bent out of shape. We can't be married or become lovers like you humans do, but with the intent and energy of humans we can join forces and merge our energies in our own special way, and this is the Inorganics' version of being mates, so to speak. You know, like Monogamy and Surrender can be."

Me: (Totally awestruck because the implications are already starting to sink in) "So what...how did you...what brought on this decision?"

Friendship: "You did in a way. You and others like you."

Romance: "Yup."

Me: "Me? How did I bring this on?"

Friendship: "Let's just say that this is inevitability that both Romance and I have seen coming for many years now. The fact that you showed up when you did and started writing a book about the possibility of our merger only convinced us that this was the omen we were looking for. So we realized after our last meeting that the time had come to cement the deal, and here we are."

Me: "Wow, this is absolutely fabulous, so what will this mean to the world and to people in general? I can only imagine that it will mostly be good."

Romance: "Yep, that is certainly the idea."

Friendship: "It will certainly be interesting, no doubt about it."

Me: "So tell me what the most significant first change might be?"

Friendship: "Hmm…that's a difficult question to answer, but let me tell you what I think."

Me: "Yes, yes, please do."

Friendship: (To herself) "Okay, how do I start? (She thinks it over then speaks again and looks directly at me.) I know you remember what it is like to fall deeply, head over heels in love with a woman, even though I know it has been a long time since you have lost yourself to that type of emotion, correct?"

Me: "Oh yes, I remember it like it was only yesterday…well…okay, maybe like it was last week or last month, but I certainly know the feelings well and I have no trouble conjuring them up."

Friendship: "Okay, good, you're with me here. Now close your eyes for a moment and recall that feeling completely and the person who evoked those feelings from you. Let the intensity of those feelings flow over you again and let them burn in you like they did the first time you felt them."

Me: (I close my eyes and let myself get into the process) "Okay, I'm there. Wow, I had forgotten how intense this feels."

Friendship: "All right, now open your eyes and let the feeling stay with you for a bit."

Me: "It's an interesting sensation to conjure those feelings up."

Romance: "I'm around that kind of energy and those types of feelings all of the time."

Me: "That must be interesting."

Friendship: "What's the longest those types of intense feelings have lasted for you when directed at any one person?"

Me: (Biting the inside of my lip while I think) "That's difficult to say, but I am sure it was months and maybe even longer."

Friendship: "So what would you say if we told you that those feelings could last years, perhaps decades, if handled appropriately?"

Me: "Wow, you mean like a long slow burn, instead of a hot and furious meltdown?"

Friendship: "Precisely."

Romance: "You see? We know that people fall into infatuation every day, but a genuine and deep abiding love is something that rarely has a chance to develop and flourish. People dive head first into the feelings of infatuation and burn hot and fast, then fizzle out so quickly. And then within months or years, depending on their individual recovery rates, they are right back at it, but telling themselves they now know how to burn hot and fast, but make it last this time. The most obvious examples of this are public figures like movie stars and rock stars who are suddenly together everywhere they go, and who get each other's names tattooed on their butts and breasts, then just as suddenly they are no longer together. Good thing they have laser removal systems for tattoos these days, huh?

Me: "I guess so, but how does your merger with Friendship change all of this?"

Friendship: "It doesn't really change it as much as it opens the door to other possibilities. Because no matter what people tell themselves, burning hot and fast is not something that people can maintain for any extended period of time. The hotter and faster they burn, the sooner the flame burns out, because it takes an immense amount of fuel to burn a big hot fire. And sooner or later that fuel is going to be exhausted and people are going to have to retreat from one another for replenishment. And fires that burn hot and fast have very little staying power for the retreat of their partners in flame."

Romance: *"That's right, but people become addicted to those feelings of infatuation easily and sooner or later they will want to burn again, hot and fast with someone new."*

Me: *"Yeah, this reminds me of my buddy Jake, who is always quoting a line from the movie* Blade Runner. *The plot is about organically engineered humans that have a very short time to live, so they want to have their creator fix the problem. But what they get instead is advice and are told that 'the flame that burns twice as bright burns half as long...so revel in your time', and then they die."*

Friendship: *"There is little difference between intense infatuations and running a marathon when it comes to the expenditure of energy; eventually you are going to run out of gas and, therefore, momentum."*

Romance: *"But this is where Friendship and I come in, because the acceptance of our merger means that people can burn hot and slow, without having to crash and smolder when they run out of fuel, which will in turn allow them to prolong the ecstasy of their intimacy and romance indefinitely."*

Me: *"What about nasty breakups? Will your merger help to counteract this problem as well?"*

Romance: *"Sure, if a couple has built their relationship on friendship it will."*

Friendship: *"Friends don't 'divorce' or 'break up' in the traditional sense. What good friends usually do is discuss their differences like adults and then simply make adjustments that are more suitable to their friendship."*

Me: *"Okay, cool, I'm buying into this, no problem, so how does it work?"*

"Every morning in Africa, a gazelle wakes up.
It knows it must outrun the fastest lion or it will be killed.
Every morning in Africa, a lion wakes up.
It knows it must run faster than the slowest gazelle, or it will starve.
It doesn't matter whether you are a lion or a gazelle;
when the sun comes up, you'd better be running."
~Unknown ~

Friendship: "You'd better type all of this directly into your computer because it is important that you don't miss a thing we are about to share with you, and the only way you'll be able to pass this information on to your readers is if you get it down and present it correctly."

Me: "Okay, I'll be right back." (I jump up and run out to the Jag to fetch my laptop.)

Romance: "The most important thing to start with, Richard, is to take your own advice and to use all of the avenues available to meet women and to make friends with them."

Friendship: (Acknowledging Romance's instructions) "That's correct. Learning how to be friends with a variety of women without having to get into their pants is a major coup for the average skirt-chasing male. (She eyes me teasingly to let me know she means males like me.) As an ambitious male, which I know you to be, it is also important to make friends with women who are more accomplished in the fields of interest in which you are attempting to achieve high levels of proficiency. And it doesn't matter if the women are much older than you or much younger. What matters is that you find women with whom you can relate, respect and honor. Then you need to learn to love and cherish these women and your friendship with them, without any expectations or demands.

Me: "And what do I tell my readers when they ask me about the importance of this specific endeavor?"

Friendship: "You tell them two things. The first is that their ability to love, honor and respect these women without any reservation, expectation or demand will empower them to do the same with women they would normally sell their hearts and souls to be with. And the second thing you tell them is that these women will be there for them at those crucial moments in life when their love and support will matter most and will be the most meaningful."

Romance: "And romancing these women is a blast because it is a different type of romance that doesn't require any return or specific reaction from them. You can wine and dine them and openly share just how much you love and enjoy their company and friendship without waiting for a similar response in kind. Trust me on this one, because there is no position more powerful with women than the ability to love them freely and openly without any prospect of reciprocation."

Friendship: "When men learn to love women—truly love them as people and not just as mates or sex partners—they will have as many close women friends as male friends, and the world will be forever brighter and unbelievably satisfying."

Me: "You know the merchant thinking of immediate return on investment that the social mind requires of us will have a serious conflict with this idea and practice."

Friendship: "Yes, we are fully aware of this, but it changes nothing. If men want to recapture their power and eventually find themselves enjoying the types of relationships with women they'd most like to have, they'd better learn this vital lesson as quickly as possible."

Me: "Wow, it doesn't sound like there is much room for debate on this issue."

Friendship: "There isn't. This is an unalterable maneuver that men will have to adopt eventually, so the sooner they get with it the better."

Romance: "Once men find out what a blast it is to have multiple women in their lives whom they can wine, dine and love with genuine abandon it will change them and their destinies forever. And this means that I'll also be able to spread my wings to new realms and go there with them."

Friendship: "The more open to friendship the men become, the more likely they will cross paths with women of like minds who would be more than happy to share physical intimacy with them as well, with little or no pursuit or coercion either."

Me: *"It might be difficult for a lot of men with strong predatory inclinations to accept the idea of sex coming to them instead of them having to chase and trap it."*

Romance: *"Ha! You know the old saying, 'Be careful what you ask for'. Well here it is."*

Me: *"Women are terribly hooked on passion these days and are often quick to dump a guy if they don't feel it for him, even when they think he is a great guy."*

Romance: *"When a guy is really aware of his skills and enjoys his predatory nature without letting it run him, he can create lots of passion in women."*

Friendship: *"Chasing down a genuine friendship with the women they really enjoy spending time with will go far in serving guys' predatory natures, because the majority of their strategic energies can eventually be focused here, along with career and other such endeavors. But it's the guy's sense of security, confidence and loving detachment that gives rise to passion."*

Me: *"I can only imagine what it might be like if millions of men suddenly started approaching millions of women just for friendship. Do you think the women who know us may all believe that we've all lost our minds?"*

Romance: *"Who cares? They'll get over it and they'll learn to love it too. (He stops and thinks for a moment, then adds an afterthought) Well, most of them will love it anyway."*

Me: *"What about all those offended men who are still licking their wounds and protecting their past injuries?"*

Friendship: *"Good question, and I have an equally good answer. Tell your male readers that they need to seriously consider and then act on the* *exploration of organizations that are traditionally oriented toward women, but happily accept and encourage the presence and membership of men. Your good friend Lynn Andrews* has a perfect organization for this very type of undertaking. She has a school which is and has been attended by thousands of women and she is a best selling author who has written at least eighteen books that would give men an unprecedented look into the psyche of the female. If your male readers are at all sincere in their desire to form the kinds of relationships with women they'd most like to have, they really ought to read her books and participate in her retreats and school."*

Romance: "Yeah, Richard, I saw you at Lynn's annual Joshua Tree retreat and you were surrounded by a sea of women. There were literally hundreds of them all around you."

Me: "Hey, hey, hey, you're going to give away my best kept secrets."

Romance: "What? And now you don't want to share?"

Me: "I love it when the women outnumber the men like that, but I admit that men who are looking to build friendships with women would be really smart to attend her retreats and school. They could easily and quickly meet and befriend more women than they thought possible, and they are women who are from all over the world."

"And for power to come to you,
you must make a place within yourself for that power to live."
~ Lynn V. Andrews ~

Friendship: "Once the action of befriending women is put into motion, men will have to learn how to deal with the consequences of their actions, because if they are smart they will have initiated more female friendships than they can possibly maintain, and will continue to do so. Since women are likely to come and go during this process the men will want to continue it until they have reached their maximum of good, close, stable friendships."

Me: "How will they know what female friends are the best ones to keep and which ones are probably best to let go?"

* http://www.lynnandrews.com

Romance: "The women decide that themselves."

Me: "How's that?"

Friendship: "The women who are the best candidates to keep as friends are the women who participate in the friendship. If they don't participate then it is probably wise to let them go."

Me: "That's almost the total opposite of what a lot of men actually do."

Romance: "Tell me about it! (He starts to chuckle at me) I can't even begin to count the number of women over the years who have actively shown interest in you, Richard, and you basically ignored them to chase women who wouldn't give you the time of day."

Me: (A little chagrined) "Yeah, yeah, I know, I know, so can we please leave me out of this?"

Romance: "(Playfully defiant) "Nope, not likely."

Me: "Geeesh, see what I get for promising to quote you guys?"

Friendship: "Well, think about it. How many of the women who tried to participate with you are still in your life?"

Me: "Uh...well, a few of them, I guess."

Romance: "And how many of the women are still in your life who you overtly pursued, but who didn't give you any real warmth or attention while you dated them?"

Me: "Uh...let's see, uh...basically none."

Romance: "And there you have it."

Friendship: (Gesturing toward Romance with her thumb) "He's right, you know. The women who don't wait for you to pick up the phone and who go ahead and buy tickets to the game, theater, movies, etc., and then who take the initiative to invite you will in all probability be the better friends."

Romance: "Yeah, Alexander Bell didn't invent the telephone just for men to call women, you know?"

Me: "You know that <u>many men will get caught up in the physical appearance of the women too, and their social minds may not let them make friends with women who will be good for them over the women who won't be good for them but who look good?</u>"

Romance: (Looking at me accusingly) "Hmm? Now who do we know that might do something like that?"

Me: "Come on, I know, I know, but this isn't about me right now."

Friendship: "<u>Men are very visual creatures</u> for sure, <u>but the benefits of accepting women friends who initiate and participate are enormous compared to chasing women who don't do these things.</u> (She pauses a moment, then has a thought) Have I ever told you the Gaelic myth about the four hunters?"

Me: "No, that doesn't sound familiar."

Friendship: "It is a myth about appearances, so it fits our topic."

Me: "Okay, tell me, it sounds interesting."

Friendship: "There were four young men who decided to go hunting one day, so they packed up their weapons and set out for a part of the forest they thought they were familiar with. Since there were four of them they felt safe in numbers and didn't take many of the precautions that hunters often take, such as bringing adequate food and water along in the case of emergencies. Anyway, the young men spent the entire day walking through endless forest in search of their prey, and the less success they had in finding game, the deeper they traveled into the darkest and most unfamiliar parts of the woodland.

"Eventually, when the young men realized the day was about to end, they turned to go back the way they had come. Each thinking the other had paid closer attention to the trail they had traversed to enter the forest together, it soon became apparent that they were hopelessly lost. So as all good hunters

do, they decided to stop where they were and to build a shelter for the night. As they built their shelter and settled into it for the night they decided they would send out scouts the following day to try and pick up the trail they had left on their way in.

"For a couple of days they took their turns as scouts and went out one at a time to try and find the way they had entered into the forest, but they were having little luck and their need for water was becoming critical. Knowing they would perish if they didn't find water soon, they changed their priority and sent out one scout each day to find a source.

"On the first day of hunting for water the first young man came upon an ugly old hag who was sitting on a well. The old woman was covered with sores and lesions that were oozing pus and she smelled as vile as a smell can get. Seeing that she was sitting on the well as if to protect or guard it, the young man called out to her.

" 'Hey, old woman, I am lost with three of my friends and we are in serious need of water to survive. We have been lost for days, so would you please move aside and allow me to help myself and save my good friends?'

" 'I'll move aside and let you take all of the water you want, young man, but first you have to give me a long, deep and sensual kiss', she replied.

"Totally repulsed and annoyed at her request, the young man moved toward her to give her the kiss. But the sight and stench of the woman

overcame him and he retreated in disgust. So he returned to his friends and told them of the encounter.

"The very next day, the second scout ventured out from the shelter and he too came across the same old woman sitting on the well. And he too asked the old woman to move aside so he could help himself to the water and save himself and his friends. As she had done the day before, she made the proposition to the second young man and asked him for a long, deep and sensual kiss. But like his friend before, his repulsion got the best of him and he returned empty-handed to his friends.

"When the third day came the situation had, of course, become desperate, so the third young man set out with a new resolve to achieve what the first two men could not. And like his friends before him, he came across the same old woman who made him the same offer she had made to his friends. But just like his buddies in the previous two days, the grotesqueness of the woman overwhelmed him and he was unable to follow through and fulfill her request.

"On the fourth day all hope had fallen to the fourth young man as he set out to find the old woman and the well. By following the marked path his three friends had left in the three days prior, the fourth young man quickly found his way to the old woman and her well.

"'Old woman', he cried out desperately to her, 'I have great need of your water to save my friends. They cannot possibly live another day without it'.

"And again the hideous old woman made the same offer to this young man that she had made to the previous three.

"'You can have all of the water you want, young man, but first you must give me a long, deep, and passionate kiss.'

"'Old woman', the young man responded to her, 'if you give me what I need to save my friends, I will not only kiss you, but I will gladly embrace you and grant any gift I am able to give'.

"As the young man approached the old woman, she began to appear less and less repulsive with every step until he finally reached her and took her in his arms. As he embraced her and prepared to kiss the woman he couldn't believe his eyes while she suddenly transformed herself into a beautiful young princess. Thinking that he must be delusional from the lack of food and water, gratefully and gently, the young man placed his lips on hers and closed his eyes while he embraced and kissed her passionately. When he suddenly heard clapping and cheering from all around him, he opened his eyes with a jerk and found himself in a huge and beautiful palace, surrounded by hundreds of people and tables that were covered in food and drink. Beside

him stood his three companions from the forest who were dressed in expensive and exquisite garb, and they looked as confused as he was.

"'You have broken the curse', the now-beautiful young woman said to him, 'and I have married you and made you king of all the lands."

Friendship stopped talking and looked at me.

Me: "Wow, some story."

Romance: "Yeah, and it is based on a true story too."

Me: "No way!"

Romance: "Yup!"

Me: "Really?"

Romance: "Yes, really. It is not exactly what happened, of course, because stories change as they are passed down through the ages. But I was there at that wedding and it is close enough."

Me: "Amazing."

Friendship: "You see, Richard, things are not always as they appear and it's not so wise to blow off someone just because she may not be as beautiful as you might like her to be."

Romance: "Average looking women are often your best gems."

Friendship: "Beauty is nice, but it often comes at a very high price for most men."

Me: "In my own experience, I have found that truly beautiful women do not always participate well, because they have become so accustomed to being pursued and to holding the power."

Romance: "It's really true. Women who participate from the outset are much more likely to be far better friends and lovers too, because they are interested and motivated."

Friendship: "And they are likely to respect your space and privacy too, but I admit that this isn't always the case."

Me: "You know, I have really learned to appreciate and value the friends I have who are not obtrusive and who respect my space."

Romance: "I guess this brings up the next point." (He looks at Friendship for permission to go on.)

Friendship: "Continue."

Romance: "It is really important for friends to respect each other's space, and I don't care how physical the relationship has become. Under no circumstances is it okay for a guy to unexpectedly stop by a woman's home, place of business, etc., unless she has given explicit permission for this to occur, and it is not okay for her to do this to a guy either. There is nothing romantic or beneficial about this type of behavior and it usually only demonstrates a person's possessiveness and insecurity."

Friendship: "It doesn't matter how good a friendship you have created or even how many times you may have been sexual with a woman; she is not your property and you have no rights to her private space unless she specifically offers them."

Me: "I've had that happen to me in recent years and I ended up having to end the friendships because the women continued to justify the behavior no matter what I said. I felt badly about it too because I liked them, but if I were to let it go on it would have only reinforced the behavior and I could have counted on it reoccurring."

Friendship: (Nodding her head in agreement) "A person's home and personal space are the only privacy they really have, so it is not okay to violate this space and privacy for any reason."

**"You must learn from the mistakes of others.
You can't possibly live long enough to make them all yourself."
~ Sam Levenson ~**

Me: "So what secrets does a man need to know to effectively maintain a solid relationship with his women friends, especially after he has become sexual with any of them?"

Romance: "I wish I could say that a little ongoing romance is all that is needed, but it's not."

Friendship: "No, it's not, but as a behavior management consultant, Richard, you already know this."

Me: "I do?"

Friendship: "Of course, you do! What is that 'three to one ratio' you are always preaching about?"

Me: "Oh, yeah, you mean about being more positive than negative?"

Friendship: "Exactly! There are always going to be things about other people that we don't find very pleasant, but to focus on these things will only serve to accentuate the negative."

Romance: "Yeah, how do you like it when a woman is always reminding you about the personal attributes you have that annoy her?"

Me: "Ugh! I'm sick of that. My friend Margaret does that to me from time to time. She tries to call it 'communicating' or 'sharing', but what she is really doing is complaining and then trying to justify it. If it were something new, I might be open to listening, but it is always just a rehashing of the same old beefs over and over."

Friendship: "Well, women don't like to hear the same complaints over and over again either, so tell your male readers to focus on the positive if they really want to keep these women in their lives."

Romance: "No matter what the woman does or doesn't do, try to find three positive things about her to focus on and to use as an offsetting balance for each one of the negatives. If men train themselves to focus on three positives for every negative they will eventually and naturally stop focusing on the negatives completely."

Friendship: (Nodding toward Romance) "He doesn't mean the negatives go away, he just means that they take a backseat and become less and less prominent. And once they take a backseat to all of the positives, they begin to matter very little until they don't matter at all. By modeling this unconditional regard and acceptance, men set themselves up to receive it in return."

Me: "So every time I start to focus on a female friend's negative behavior or impact on me, I need to stop myself and counter this thought by finding three positives about her that I like and focus on those?"

Friendship: "That's correct, and then decide if these positives really outweigh the negatives or not. I think you will find that most of the time they do."

Romance: "Then make it a point to express your appreciation in some manner to the woman for having and sharing these positive attributes."

"Winners have simply formed the habit
of doing things losers don't like to do."
~ Albert Gray ~

Me: "I have another issue I want to ask about."

Friendship: "Okay, what?"

Me: (Biting my inner lip and trying to think carefully about how to express my thought) "It has been my experience that women, in general, prefer to find men who are at least a match for themselves and who are more secure and not easily bent or pushed around. And they often lose respect for men they can bend to their will or can otherwise walk on and push around."

Romance: "Well, yeah...That's not a big revelation; so what?"

Me: "Then why is it that when they do find a guy like this, they spend the next century trying to bend him and push him around anyway? I mean, why can't they just be happy with their good fortune and achievement?"

210

Both Friendship and Romance burst out laughing at the same time, roll their eyes at me and nudge each other with their knees and elbows.

Me: "Okay, okay, what's so damn funny?"

Romance: "You are, of course."

Friendship: "Look, Richard, how do you know your car is going to start every day, or your radio is going to work when you want to listen to it, or that your computer is going to boot up when you want to write?"

Me: "I have to turn the ignition and start the car or flip the buttons to the 'on' position to see if the electronics fire up to know for sure."

Romance: "Well, women are no different than you. They don't know if you are really working correctly or not until they hit your ignition switch to see if you 'fire up' as well."

Both Romance and Friendship start to laugh again, so I wait until they settle down.

Me: "Okay, I see your point, but how many years does this take, especially if I am already modeling the confidence and self-security they prefer to see anyway?"

Friendship: "It just depends on the woman, Richard, so get over it already. As long as you aren't engaging in a power struggle with her, who cares?"

Romance: "Yeah, it's not personal anyway, so don't take it personally and get over it. Just imagine you have a tiger by the tail and stay the hell out of the way of its claws and jaws."

They burst out laughing again and nudge each other like they have a private joke going on between them.

Friendship: "I'll tell you one thing for certain; if you do find a woman who just accepts you as you are and who doesn't waste her time and yours in constant challenges and battles, do whatever you have to do to hang on to her, because she is most definitely a keeper."

Me: "Okay, that sounds like really good advice, but what do you mean by 'engaging in a power struggle' with women?"

Romance: "The struggle for emotional dominance between two people."

Friendship: "You know, she goes out with some other guy to make you jealous, then you get even by going out to make her jealous; or she disappears for a while and then you disappear; or she screws some other guy and rubs your nose in it, or you screw some other woman and rub her nose in it, etc., until it turns into a vicious game and cycle of tit for tat. Some people do this just to get attention and others do it to gain the advantage. It might help to keep sex hot and interesting over the years, but it is not love or affection."

Me: "No, I don't get caught up in that kind of nonsense. But I know couples who have stayed together for decades because they were hooked by the power struggle."

Romance: "Maybe you're not caught up in it any longer, but you used to be because you knew it kept make-up sex hot and passionate."

Me: "Well, that's true; I used to do a lot of stupid things. But how does one know for sure when he is being a shit and when he is being an impeccable friend, because our friends are not going to like everything we do, especially when we are being sexual with them, and they are going to challenge us and our behaviors."

Friendship: "Learn to check your intent and be brutally honest with yourself. You know lots of couples in power struggles, but do they ever admit it to you or to themselves?"

Me: "Rarely."

Romance: "If you consider the true motives behind your actions, words and deeds, and you know you are trying to get a reaction, are after retribution, or want to cause hurt and pain, then you are being an asshole.

But if you can really be sincere with yourself and know that you are acting in your own best interests or in the best interests of the other, then don't worry and hold your ground. If there is no intent to do harm or to deliberately cause inconvenience or hurt of any kind, then you are probably being an impeccable friend."

Me: "So men really aren't being assholes for trying to achieve the types of relationships they most desire, even when some women find their desires to be offensive?"

Friendship: "It doesn't matter if the guy wants a traditional wife and family, or if he is Hugh Hefner with six girlfriends or sixty; and it doesn't matter if a guy likes to be the submissive waif who prefers the woman to cuff him and be in charge, as long his intent is impeccable and he honors his friends, treats them with genuine kindness and respect, then he is not an asshole and he can have any kind of relationship his little heart desires."

Romance: "There are millions and millions of women who are seeking a man to love, so the openings for being loved are endless. Do you have what it takes to accept the position and fill an opening?"

Me: "I'd like to think I do."

Romance: "Then find an opening and fill it. If she is a good friend and person, you will be building on a solid foundation."

Friendship: "Just remember to follow the four little guidelines to finding success in your friendships with women."

Me: Which are?"

Friendship: "To be kind, patient, ruthless and sweet."

Me: "Ruthless?"

Romance: "Relax, she isn't referring to meanness or to taking advantage of people."

Friendship: "No, I'm not."

Me: "Okay, what do you mean then?"

Friendship: "I can give you an example of all four guidelines with one illustration. Just imagine you are standing near the street at the end of your driveway and the neighbor's four-year old child is riding his bike down his driveway to the street. You see that a big truck is coming and that the child is about to ride right out in front of it. You know you don't have time to catch and stop him gently, so you run toward him and as you dive forward all you have time to do is to knock him to the pavement. Even though you know you are going to skin his little knees and elbows, that he'll never see the danger you are saving him from, that he'll probably be afraid of you for weeks, months or years, and that his parents might even take you to court and sue you for assaulting their kid, what are you going to do?"

Me: "Ouch. I'm going to act, in any way I can, of course, to divert death and destruction from overtaking him."

Friendship: "And then will you pick him up, dust him off, and tend to his little cuts and scratches?"

Me: "Of course!"

Friendship: "That's exactly what I mean, Richard—be kind, patient, ruthless and sweet."

**"It is not death that a man should fear,
but he should fear never beginning to live."
~ Marcus Aurelius ~**

THE LAST WORD

"A man who has never made a woman angry is a failure in life."
~ Christopher Morley ~

I was on my way back to Los Angeles from St. Croix in the U.S. Virgin Islands and had a layover in San Juan, Puerto Rico. So I went to the Marriott Resort and took my laptop to the coffee house where I could work peacefully on some strategies for affective behavioral intervention, and also watch women passing by, of course.

As I worked diligently on a new plan to reduce some specific school problems, I felt the unexpected presence of someone looking over my shoulder. It was a familiar, pleasant and calm feeling I was experiencing and I suddenly realized who it was. I turned my head to look slightly up and saw this little Native American woman looking at me with bright shiny eyes. She smiled broadly as I marveled at the power of her gaze. Her eyes were black, shiny and clear, and they exuded health and vitality. She was dressed in modern clothing, with a turquoise blouse and rather short, tight-fitting skirt and pumps, but she wore her hair in traditional braids and had native handmade jewelry hanging from her neck and wrists.

"Are you going to invite me to join you?" she finally said to me in some native tongue, and it broke my fixation on her incredible eyes.

"Yes, yes," I finally stuttered back, as I lifted halfway out of my chair.

"Sit still," she replied to me with words that seemed to pop in my head like exploding soap bubbles, and she put her hand on my arm as she moved to take the chair right next to me.

The Spirit of Peace always appeared to me as a warm, attractive female who was native to whatever country I happened to be in and I was always thrilled to see her, but I never quite comprehended how I was always able to understand her when she spoke to me in a language I wasn't familiar with. When I questioned her she always explained it as a part of my "dreaming" process and said that she was able to tap into it. She said it was similar to the function of me reading her thoughts, and of her reading mine, or more appropriately, that we were entering each other's dreams. But whatever it was, it was a strange sensation like instantly knowing something without a reason why. And the sensation of hearing her voice, or thoughts, was similar to having a series of sudden realizations without knowing from where they came.

Me: "It's nice to see you, Peace. It has been a while."

Peace: "Did you miss me, Richard?"

Me: "Of course I did, I always miss you when I don't feel you with me."

Peace: "Well, you know you could have me around more often if you really wanted? In fact, you could have me around all of the time. It is really up to you."

Me: "I know you tell me this quite often, but I am not certain how I constantly lose touch with you."

Peace: (Smiling coyly at me) "Oh, come on now."

Me: "It's strange how I feel you one minute, but not the next. And I did what you told me to do; I examined what I was thinking about when I lost touch."

Peace: "And?"

Me: "And I have always let my thoughts and mood drift off to something unpleasant."

Peace: "See? You know exactly what happens to you."

Me: "*But sometimes I am not really thinking about anything at all.*"

Peace sat quietly for a few minutes and looked right through me with those piercing eyes. When her words starting popping into my head again, it was as if she had been reading my thoughts for weeks, and was now taking the opportunity to respond to them:

Peace: "*When we live our lives in conflict with our dreams, this behavior sabotages both our mental and physical health, so we constantly have to be on guard against the preprogrammed dictates of the social mind that most often causes this destructive behavior.*"

Her words made me feel guilty and a little self-conscious. I knew exactly what she was talking about, but I had to ask as if I didn't:

Me: "*Are you referring to something specific?*"

Peace: "*Come on, Richard, you are a bright boy. There is no need to act innocent with me, because you know I won't pass judgment on you.*"

Me: "*I can't seem to help myself, Peace. I always seem to want more than I get and I never seem to be happy when I finally get what I want.*"

Peace: "*That's because the answer to your prayers rarely shows up in the form you think it will.*"

Me: "*You got that right.*"

Peace: "*I know that your personal power brings numerous women your way. One gives you one thing and another gives you something different, so I don't see what the problem is.*"

Me: "*The problem is how long it seems to take to for someone to finally break though the barriers of the social mind and just enjoy what I am able to give, without constantly trying to fix or change me.*"

Peace: "*You're talking about women like Serge's ex-wife, isn't that so?*"

Me: "How can I ever convince men to accept women and maintain a friendship bond with them when they can be so damn hardheaded?"

Peace: "As long as men like Serge don't have a need to press their agenda, it shouldn't be a problem."

My buddy Serge dated and then lived with a woman named Rita for a few years who was on a mission to get married. Whenever they would take weekends away or extended vacations, Rita would wait until they were into their trip and would then spend the entire time verbally pounding on Serge to come around to her marital way of thinking. Serge, on the other hand, was happy being single and he enjoyed his exciting and interesting life. He had no desire to be married, but he loved Rita deeply and wanted her to stay with him and invited her to move in. After accepting his invitation and moving into his place, Rita eventually quit her job and worked with him too, so their lives became completely enmeshed.

Rita knew that Serge had been single for many years and that he had no desire or need to get hitched. He was honest with her about his feelings on marriage from the very beginning, but she was resolute in her goal. And the power struggle over their definitive journey to the future as a couple took precedence over everything else. Ultimately, Rita tried a number of strategies and she took the battle to many of Serge's friends and family members, especially the females, and was able to recruit a number of them to badger him on her behalf. "Well, if you really love her," a number of them would say, "then you should marry her." But Serge was resolute too and stood his ground because he didn't want to be badgered into a life he hadn't chosen voluntarily. As the pressure on Serge began to mount he found himself running from it by accepting more contracts and work in other cities and states where he hoped he could get some peace. What he failed to consider was the fact that other cities and states also had telephones and that any conversations with Rita would always be focused on her favorite topic.

Eventually, Rita waited until she and Serge were together on a weekend getaway to announce that she had had enough, that she had met another man, and was moving to an apartment the new guy had rented for her. Although she would be hard-pressed to admit it to this day, this was again another ploy in the power struggle designed to bring Serge under her control. The resulting effect for Serge, however, was relief from the unrelenting pressure and an even stronger determination to hold his ground and not be intimidated. As realization quickly set in that her plot hadn't reaped the expected results, Rita promptly returned to reconcile and requested forgiveness for her thoughtless misjudgment. Serge loved her and immediately took her back, of course, so the power struggle resumed with zest.

While the weeks, months and years passed by, Serge began to believe that the pressure of the power struggle would never cease until Rita finally got what she wanted. He knew that giving into her might only change her focus to a different topic and struggle, but Serge was tired and longed for the serenity he once knew. So plans were finally made, the guests were all invited, and the couple was wed in true matrimonial fashion.

Just as Serge suspected, the focus and topic of the struggle took on new dimensions and where they would live and the amount of time they would spend together became the overriding issues. Serge was a computer engineer and a software designer who traveled for business and had to spend months at a time on the east coast, but Rita wanted to live in her favorite city in the west. As Rita nestled into her lovely new San Diego home and Serge catered to his Fortune 500 clients in New York, the new battleground for conflict was established, and the new mode of combat engaged.

Rita's life was good—she had the big new home she had coveted for years, she didn't have to work, and she could pursue whatever activities her little heart desired. But most of all, Rita had found a husband who loved her beyond measure and who would go to any lengths within his means, and then some, to make her life complete. The problem, of course, was Serge's absences. Serge's growing businesses required his constant attention, so he wasn't always available on demand. Never mind that Rita knew this when she picked the location of her home; never mind that Serge's businesses paid for the affluent lifestyle bequeathed to her, and never mind that Serge had sweat blood to create the businesses that funded her life. As far as Rita was concerned, his place was there with her, and he should do whatever was necessary to make it happen.

Over the course of their multi-year marriage, Rita complained incessantly about Serge's absence when he traveled and Serge complained that she couldn't be happy and just leave well enough alone. They lived a good life and enjoyed each other's company in many ways, but both of them gained weight and each of them began to suffer from bouts of reoccurring depression. Naturally, both believed deeply in their personal convictions and the justification for their individual positions, so the writing was definitely on the wall. Serge realized that divorce was on the horizon long before Rita finally brought it up, and in the end, Serge gave her everything but his business.

It has been several years since they divorced, but Rita still depends primarily on Serge for her income and Serge gladly assists her. They spend major holidays together, birthdays together, expensive vacations together, and Serge has employed her with a substantial salary since the required alimony has expired. And since the time of their divorce, their friendship has blossomed and flourished. Serge is relieved, his business continues to grow, and his overall health has returned. But for Rita, however, it is another story and the struggle with her mental and physical health continues.

For Serge very little has changed when it comes to his feelings and commitment to Rita, and he has no plans to alter them. For Rita, everything has changed and her commitment to finding a husband who meets the exact criteria of her installed social mind continues undaunted. No different than any time during their marriage, Serge is there for Rita when she needs him. But Rita places restrictions and requirements on Serge that fit the requirements of religious and social propriety and often the personal demands of her current suitor. She claims that her dream is to find a mate who offers the emotional, financial and moral support that a woman and wife deserves and is entitled to have. And while she enjoys the love, devotion, financial and emotional support of a man like Serge, she continues her search for the perfect husband, while her health is constantly in flux and frightening her.

"A positive attitude may not solve all your problems, but
it will annoy enough people to make it worth the effort."
~ Herm Albright ~

Peace: "Of all the people you know, it's your buddy Serge who could find reasons to hold a grudge, if he really wanted to."

Me: "Some say Serge is just being used and is a fool for his love and devotion. Others say he is codependent and needs to have his head examined"

Peace: "I say that Serge has his eyes wide open and knows exactly what he is doing. And I also say that Serge has learned the true art form of friendship bonding. Serge isn't sitting around waiting for Rita to come to her senses, is he?"

Me: "Oh, no! He gets around and is having a ball."

Peace: "And I doubt he is wishing for any conventional returns on his investment. He knows who Rita is and he knows that if he responds in kind and rejects her that he is only taking her deeper into the trap that has already snared her."

Me: "Yes, if he demands that she be something other than she is or to accept his agenda, he is only behaving like she does."

Peace: "Serge realizes that she may never understand the real gift he is giving her and that she may never know how he is leading her to freedom, and to me. But he also knows, beyond a shadow of a doubt, that his own salvation and freedom depend greatly upon the love that he models for those who are important to him and for all of those around him in general. And once you men free yourselves from the need to take offense, what is left is an incredible capacity for love and the acceptance of others."

Me: "Yeah, well…that's all fine and dandy, Peace, but how do I really get this message across to myself and to other men who will read my book?"

Peace: "There is a powerful and poignant story I learned from the shaman of North America, and that I teach to other shaman around the world. I like this story because it helps us realize how taking offense only serves to mask our own complicity in creating the unpleasant circumstances in our own lives. It is only one from myriad stories of Native American mythology and I have named it 'The Warrior, The Snake and The Fox'. And here is how it goes:

"An Indian warrior goes out to hunt one day in the forest. As he is walking along, he hears a terribly loud thrashing in the thicket. At first he tries to ignore the noise because he cannot tell what kind of beast is making it. But as the warrior tries to pass, his curiosity finally gets the best of him and he goes to investigate. Cautious as he can possibly be, the warrior pushes through the thick brush until he suddenly comes upon the source of the noise. In front of him and only a few feet away the warrior spots a huge snake that has gotten itself entangled and trapped in a thorny bush.

M. CORTES

Peace (cont.): "'Oh, thank goodness!' the snake said to the warrior when he saw him. 'I was beginning to lose all hope that anyone would come along who could rescue me. Won't you please give me some assistance, Mr. Warrior, and free me from this trap of nature that will cause my certain death?'

"Feeling empathy for the snake the warrior gives its request some consideration.

"'How do I know that you won't bite me once I've freed you from the brush?' the warrior asks the snake. 'I don't want to free you and be bitten for my trouble.'

"'Oh, don't be silly', the snake replied. 'Why would I bite you for saving my life? If you really think about it, you'll realize how foolish it would be for me to do such a thing to someone who has just saved me. Don't you see?'

"Clearly the snake had a point, the warrior thought. 'Why would he bite me for saving his life?' he asked himself.

"'Okay, I will help you', the warrior told him, 'but only if you'll assure me that you won't bite me once I've freed you from your trap.'

"Again the snake explained how foolish and ungrateful it would be of him to bite the Indian for saving him, and he reassured the warrior that he would never do any such thing.

"The warrior, feeling fairly confident in his agreement with the snake, laid down his weapons and began to untangle the snake's body from the brush. Carefully and gently he lifted each part of the snake's body out of the thicket until the snake was almost completely free. Then, just as the snake realized the warrior was about to accomplish the task, he opened his mouth as wide as he could and attacked the warrior with a vicious bite.

"Stunned and surprised, the warrior tried to reach for his weapons, but the snake was already on him and had already gained the advantage. Fiercely and with great courage, the warrior fought back, but as the battle raged on, it was becoming increasing clear that the snake was going to finish him.

"After what seemed like an infinitely long time, and almost totally exhausted, the warrior fell to his knees. Winding and twisting around his prey, the snake prepared to make his final assault to finish the warrior off. Then, suddenly, just as the snake was about to strike its final blow, a little fox jumped from behind a tree where it had been watching and yelled at the snake.

"'Hey Mr. Snake, what are you doing there?' the little fox called.

"Startled, the snake turned its attention toward the fox to see who was calling out to him. In an instant, the warrior realized this was the only chance he was going to get, and with all the strength he had left, he leapt towards the thicket and flung the snake back into the brush where it was trapped once again.

"Exhausted and half-dead, the warrior crawled a few feet away to a nearby tree to tend his wounds and rest. After he had rested a while and regained some of his strength he looked across at the snake.

"'Why did you do it?' he asked the snake. 'Why did you bite me and try to kill me when I had saved your life?'

"The snake looked back at the warrior as if he were totally confused by the question. After a few moments, and as if it were the most obvious answer in the world, the snake finally replied with a shrug. 'I'm a snake.'

"Later, when he could finally walk again, the warrior found the little fox who had saved him.

"'You saved my life,' he said to the little fox. 'What can I do for you to show you how much I appreciate what you've done?'

"'Oh, don't worry about it", the little fox replied. 'It's just fortunate that I happened along when I did, so feel blessed about that.'

"'No!' the warrior answered him. 'There has to be something I can do for you to repay you for your kindness and your help. Won't you please let me pay the debt that I owe you?'

"'You don't owe me anything', the little fox said. 'Besides, I'm a fox and you're a man, so there isn't anything you can do for me anyway.'

" 'But I must', the warrior demanded. 'There must be something I can do!'

"Finally, after the little fox realized the warrior was not going to acquiesce, he came up with an idea.

" 'Okay, okay', the little fox said. 'If I ever get hungry and am in need of food, then you can feed me. Will this satisfy your need to repay me?'

" 'Absolutely!' The warrior responded. 'I would be honored to share my food with you anytime you have need. Do not hesitate to call upon me!'

"Happy they had struck a bargain the warrior felt he could live with, both he and the fox went on their separate paths. Over the next several months, the warrior often thought of the little fox and wondered how he was doing. Then, late one cold winter's night, the warrior was resting in his lodge when he heard a terrible commotion out in his chicken coop. So the warrior jumped to his feet and grabbing his spear like a good protective warrior would, he ran out into the deep snow. When he got to his chicken pen, the warrior could see feathers lying around and some blood. As he got closer he saw an animal with a chicken in its mouth trying to flee from the pen. Instinctually, the warrior drew back and then thrust his arm forward, and with deadly accuracy he let his spear find its target.

"Within a moment or two, the warrior stood over the little fox he had just speared. Shocked and amazed when he discovered that it was his little friend, he stood looking down in bewilderment. As the little fox took in its final breath, he looked up at the warrior and asked him:

" 'Don't you remember the bargain we made?' "

"Our best success comes after our greatest disappointments."
~ Henry Ward Beecher ~

I sat stunned by Peace's story and all the ramifications of it swelled in my head. I could not help but see myself and many of the little foxes from my own personal history who tried to love, rescue and care for me when I needed them, and I had repaid their kindness and devotion much the same way the warrior did in this story. Maybe they weren't foxy enough, or maybe they said or did things to offend me, or maybe they were too easy and took away the challenge I thought I needed, but whatever they did or didn't do, they certainly didn't deserve my fatal response.

Finally, Peace's words started popping into my head again and they snapped me out of my reverie. It took me a moment to refocus my attention on what she was saying, but the force of her declaration brought me back to our conversation.

Peace: "Learning to take care of those who take care of us is paramount to achieving success in life and to feeling peace with ourselves."

Me: "Yeah, but I'm just like that warrior in your story."

Peace: "We all are, and so are your readers, whether they see it or not."

Me: "I remember believing that the right thing to do was to cut a woman loose when she wasn't being who I thought she should be, just like Rita has done to Serge. Sometimes I did it just because my lover didn't meet my standards for looks, and sometimes I did it just because I was a little bored, or felt like I needed to move on to something more appealing and interesting. After a few months with any woman I would always find something I didn't like about her and would move on to the next one."

Peace: "Except for those occasions when the women would break it off with you first, right?"

Me: "Yeah, and I always felt indignant too, and I rarely noticed my own behavior and reflection in those women who sent me packing."

Peace: "I remember one or two who tried to point out what you were doing and that some woman was going to do the same to you."

Me: "Yeah, I remember. Just like the warrior helping the snake, they dropped their shields of self-protection, only to have me bite them when they were the most vulnerable."

Peace: "When you act out of social conditioning, with little or no thought and understanding, you end up as part of the herd: the mindless livestock and food source for your Inorganic Masters."

Me: "There sure are a lot of wounded warriors running around out there in our world who unwittingly feed those beings."

Peace: "And they lash out at any perceived offense. So building other gender relationships are going to be difficult for them."

Me: "You mean they see women as snakes who cannot be trusted?"

Peace: "Exactly. Just look at the men who feel they have been betrayed by cheating women. They will not lay down their weapons and truly engage someone, or they drop their guard completely and end up getting bitten, time and time again. Rarely do they see their own histories reflected in their experience, and often they turn and do something similar when a woman doesn't live up to their social minds' expectations."

Me: "Wow, it is really a vicious circle, isn't it?"

Peace: "Yes, it is, and that's why so few people ever know me well."

"An eye for an eye makes the whole world blind."
~ Mahatma Gandhi ~

Me: "So what are you saying? That we should just overlook the offense?"

Peace: "I am saying that there are other choices that can be made."

Me: "Such as?"

Peace: "Well, let's take your friend Serge for an example. Instead of feeling wounded, angry and used, he decided to learn and turn this experience into an advantage."

Me: "Oh, yeah, how do you figure?"

Peace: "Isn't Rita one of his best friends now?"

Me: "Yes, she certainly is."

Peace: "So, he has a woman he deeply loves as one of his closest allies and he has relations with other women too, does he not?"

Me: "Okay, good point, he really does have the best of both worlds, but how do you convince a guy that he should overlook something like betrayal and rejection?"

Peace: "A man can certainly expect a snake to be a snake, so there is no need to be offended when a snake behaves the way that snakes behave; and it is the same with people. As experienced, evolving warriors, it is your duty as men to learn to deal with the world of people and Inorganic Beings without becoming their victim."

"Mankind censure injustice fearing that they may be the victims of it, and not because they shrink from committing it."
~ Plato ~

****

It is always cold in Kansas when I go to spend the year-end holiday season with my family. I never liked the chill of winter when I was growing up there and I still don't like it now, but being with my family through nearly all of December has become more of a treat than ever. With two young athletic brothers who both play basketball in Kansas, I can't wait for the chance to go and watch them demonstrate their prowess on the court. Win or lose, it doesn't really matter, because the magic of those brief events in time has become a priceless commodity for me. Youth disappears so quickly that there is little time to savor it and to enjoy the passing of its brilliance.

I suppose the wintry setting of Kansas City was a most appropriate environment for another specific visitor to join me, because cold always accompanies his presence wherever he goes. In fact, he is known for his coldness and there is no way to avoid the distinct chill of its touch while in his company. I was killing some time in the Westport District of Kansas City, Missouri, after dropping a friend at the airport when I decided to stop and have some breakfast. I had another appointment in the Plaza which is nearby to Westport, but it was still too early to go. I knew of a quaint little breakfast house named First Watch in the strip center on the corner of Westport Boulevard and Southwest Trafficway, so I decided to go there.

When I walked in the restaurant I went to the hostess' station and stood immediately behind a tall, impeccably dressed black man in a finely tailored, navy blue pin-striped suit. He looked like he was in his mid to late forties and very successful. As I stood near him I could feel his energy and I could instantly tell that he was a very powerful being. I saw him glance at me as I walked up behind him, so I gave him a nod. He didn't acknowledge my subtle greeting at all and ignored me completely until the hostess walked up to seat him. "How many in your party?" she asked him as she grabbed at menus from a stack to her right. "One," he said, and then hesitated to follow the hostess while looking at me. "Are you going to join me?" he asked with cool indifference before he took a step to walk away.

I looked at him dumbfounded for a moment until I finally realized who he was. I was certainly familiar with the cool indifference of Death, but this was the first time he had appeared to me as he was. "I'll join him," I said to the hostess and she grabbed another menu and walked us to a booth.

A cute little blond showed up quickly to take our order before we could talk. I ordered two eggs over-easy, bacon, toast, and hash browns with lots of extra sautéed onions on them, and coffee. Death just asked for coffee.

Me: "I wasn't expecting to see you just yet?" (I say more as a question than a statement.) "But I knew this meeting was coming."

Death just looked at me with cold dark eyes and offered no explanation or response of any kind.

Me: "Why here, why now?"

Death: "You're the one who summoned me." (He says this very matter-of-fact.)

Me: "Actually, I have been avoiding you, but I was hoping not to have to deal with you until next month."

Death: "Most people want to put me off and wait until next month, next year, or forever, but how will that help you?"

Me: "It doesn't, but I've put you off for several years already, so what's another month?"

Death's eyes were incredibly dark and piercing. When we made eye contact I felt the cold chill of his look run through my entire body like a mild current of electricity shooting down my veins to the tips of my toes.

Death: "Sooner or later you are going to have to face me and deal with your commitment. The longer you take the sooner I'll gain the upper hand for good and there will be no stopping me. I'll come to take you entirely and long before you have accomplished your goals."

Me: "You have been a reliable consultant and advisor for many years now, but you still want a part of me that is incredibly difficult for me to surrender, even though I am not afraid."

Death: "I am the best advisor any man or woman could have. I tell it exactly like it is."

"Death is a friend of ours;
and he that is not ready to entertain him is not at home."
~ Sir Francis Bacon ~

Me: "Then why am I still so damn reluctant to give in and let the fat Richard die, once and for all?"

Death: "You know the answer already and you just want to whine about it. You have been the fat Richard for decades and the fat Richard has a life of his own, just like any man has a life. The fat Richard has feelings, habits, clothing, likes, dislikes, and is your most dependable source of indulgence and immediate gratification."

We were interrupted by a different waitress who brought my food and the coffee pot to refill our cups. She was a cute little brunette in her late twenties or early thirties with longish hair tied back, perky full breasts, and a tight, firm little butt wrapped up in skintight pants. She fit a lot of the pictures I have in my head of what I'm immediately attracted to physically. Death watched me check out the waitress' butt as she walked away. I brought my attention back to the table and picked up my toast to cover it with strawberry preserves.

Death: "There's a good example of what I'm talking about."

I stopped spreading preserves on my toast and looked at him.

Death: "You know you could have as many of those as you want (nodding his head and casting his eyes toward the waitress that just walked away). Even better-looking than she is, if you would let the fat Richard die."

I considered his words for a moment, then went back to arranging my food. I laid the two slices of toast on my plate, preserve side up, and then carefully laid two slices of bacon on each slice of toast. Then I took my two over-easy eggs and covered the bacon on each slice of toast with them to make two open faced sandwiches. I broke the yoke underneath each egg so the bread could soak it up and the yoke wouldn't be lost on my plate. After that I put a little ketchup on my hash browns and mixed it in with the sautéed onions. I picked up my knife and fork and cut a bite from one of the bacon, egg and toast piles I'd just created. It almost melted in my mouth as I began to chew.

Death: "You even make love to your food."

Me: (Taking a big bite of hash browns) "Yeah, I know it."

Death: "I bet you say goodbye to your turds before you flush them, then wave to them as they go down the drain."

Me: (Sarcastically) "Yeah, I give them each names too. Okay, I admit I love food, but I'm not that bad."

Death looks at me for a moment, then slides out of the booth and stands up.

Death: "I'll meet you tomorrow in Topeka at the coffee house. Right now, I have something else to do and you're giving too much attention to your food."

Without another word Death turned and walked out of the restaurant. I was tempted to feel a little insulted, but I knew it was a waste of my time and energy, so I quickly let go of the urge and finished eating my meal. The presence of Death had always affected my mood and my energy level. Whenever I had to deal with him I always felt somewhat morose and drained.

The next morning, I met my teenaged brother at the gym in Topeka and we did an early workout. I planned to meet my father later at his favorite sandwich shop for a late lunch, but in the meantime I needed to check my e-mails and see if Death was really going to show up. I drove over to the World Cup Coffee House at twenty-first and Washburn where I can always hook up my laptop to a high-speed cable connection and relax on a big comfortable sofa with a hot mug of java. The World Cup is a very comfortable and friendly environment that also makes a great ham and cheese sandwich they call "The Hot One." When I arrived, I grabbed a mug of hazelnut decaf and immediately claimed my favorite sofa.

A few minutes after I was comfortable and busy responding to e-mail, I noticed a big fat guy come in. I could see him from the corner of my eye, lumbering across the floor. I was vaguely aware of him as he went to the counter and ordered a coffee and a "Hot One." He paid his bill, then walked toward my area of the store as if every step was painful and he couldn't bear to carry the weight of his body. Without any fanfare he plopped his fat butt down on the overstuffed chair across from me. I glanced up briefly to look at him and he was staring directly at me. His look was cold and unfriendly, so I went back to work without really acknowledging him. He was a Caucasian man who looked to be in his late fifties, with short brown unkempt hair, dark withdrawn eyes, a huge middle of fat rolls, heavily blemished skin, and a strong, semi-unpleasant odor. Within seconds he broke the silence I was hoping he would honor and I knew as soon as he spoke that he was Death.

Death: "This is what is going to happen to you if you don't stop eating the way you do."

I stopped working on my e-mails, closed my laptop, sat it on the ottoman in front of me, and then looked at him. I knew he was right about me, but I always think I have more time to get my stuff together than I really do.

Me: "You know that I have to starve the fat Richard to death if I really want to kill him off? And that doesn't really strike me as a very pleasant experience, although I've done it many times before."

Death: "You've certainly managed to lean down and become very trim at intervals in your life, but you've never killed off the fat Richard once and for all. He keeps making a comeback because you feel sorry for him."

Me: "Starving him is starving me, so he really does have a life of his own, doesn't he?"

Death: *"Of course he does. He wakes up every morning looking forward to his day and to the good foods he is going to indulge himself with. He has had a long life that includes an education, family, love, sex, work, a home, and everything else that makes a man have a rich, full and complete life. And every time you try to let him go and starve him to death, he begs you not to do it."*

Me: *"It's that way with everybody, isn't it? No matter who we are or what we want that part of ourselves that keeps us from our dreams must die."*

Death: *"Yes."*

Me: *"Is this the reason that most people never achieve their dreams or change their behaviors?"*

Death: *"Of course it is. Who willingly and knowingly goes to his death?"*

Me: *"So how do people give up the selves that cause them misery when the miserable self is the only self they have ever really known? People keep doing the same things over and over again with the same disastrous results."*

Death: "Are you referring primarily to people who continue to form and repeat disastrous relationships?"

Me: "Yes, of course, because this is important information I need to share with my readers. And I think we've covered more than enough about me and my personal shortcomings for the moment."

A young high school or college-aged girl brings the ham and cheese sandwich Death ordered when he came in the coffee house. She looks at him and he points at me, so the girl hands me the sandwich.

Death: "Go ahead; I know that's one of your favorites here."

I knew he did that just to mess with me and to make a point about my weakness for food.

Death: "So what are you asking me specifically?"

Me: "Men and women still believe that when they couple up or marry they belong to each other like property. And more times than not, this attitude causes a devastating ending. There is a multibillion-dollar divorce industry out there, complete with law offices all over the world, which thrives on the anger, hate, disappointment, jealousy and conflict that occurs as a result of relationships gone sour. But people keep recreating these fruitless conditions and fragile relationships over and over again."

Death: "It doesn't matter if someone is addicted to tobacco, alcohol, drugs, gambling, sex, physical abuse, or any other unhealthy vice. The price of freedom is the same for everyone, and that price is me."

"Death is the mother of Beauty; hence from her, alone,
shall come fulfillment to our dreams and our desires."
~ Wallace Stevens ~

Me: "So you're telling me that any major change in life direction requires a form of death?"

Death: "More or less."

Me: "But everyone is afraid of you."

Death stops talking for a few minutes and burns a hole through me with his eyes. He appears to be considering something carefully before he speaks again.

Death: "Imagine a point in this room about eye level and five feet out in front of you. Imagine this point is about the size of a pinpoint and that it has lines emanating from it in every conceivable direction, like light beams emanating from the sun in every direction."

Me: "Okay, I've got it."

Death: "As you can tell, the number of directions that are possible from that tiny point is almost endless. Move the point over a fraction of an inch and you have an entirely new set of endless directions. Move the point again and another endless set of directions is possible and so on. These endless numbers of directions originated from the Big Bang event and the endless lines of direction are the source of the 'strings' in the 'Super String Theory', currently being explored by your physicists like Stephen Hawking and John Hagelin."

Me: "Wow, I have read Dr. Hawking's book A Brief History of Time *where I first learned about the 'String Theory'."*

Death: "Inorganic Beings call these directional strings the 'lines of the world', because they mark the boundaries of other worlds and directions to other worlds. In the places where these lines are concentrated into massive bundles are where the concentration of matter is, such as planets, stars and nebulae. And these concentrations of matter are a product of a massive concentration of thought. These lines cause our universe to be layered much like an onion is, with layers of worlds upon worlds, upon worlds."

Me: "Monogamy showed me some of those layers using mirrors. And I think I stepped across a few of those lines in the process."

Death: "You did, and you can step across those lines from any point in life as well. <u>No matter where you are, or at what point ~~you~~ of life you are in, there are an endless set of directions to choose from. Pick any direction you want and there will be a different world and future on that path.</u> If you live in the world known as Denver and decide to go south to the world known as Albuquerque, the future will be different than it would if you had gone east to the world of Kansas City. Or, if you go north to Cheyenne the future would be different than if you had gone west to Salt Lake City. And none of these places are within view of the other, so the future in each is an unknown. Once you get to Albuquerque or to Cheyenne, you have a whole new set of directions to choose from again."

"The great thing in this world is not so much where you stand, as in what direction you are moving."
~ Oliver Wendell Holmes ~

Me: "But how can you call these different worlds?"

Death: "Because they are. Do you really think the housewife who wakes up in New York is going to travel the same routes, see the same people and have the same life routines as the housewife who wakes up in Los Angeles, or the housewife who wakes up in Sydney, or in Beirut?"

<u>Me</u>: "<u>Okay, I get it. If I want to be a lean man I have to choose the direction to that world and go to live in it, correct</u>? And the future will be different than it would have been for the world of the fat man."

Death: (Very matter-of-fact) "Yes. And the route to the lean Richard requires the death of the fat one."

Me: "But how does that help me accept the death of the fat man? Or anyone else accept the death of the drug addict, the wife abuser, or whatever else they may have always been?"

Death: "Which life do you most desire?"

Me: "It should be a choice as easy as that."

Death: "⬛ *Death is like crossing the horizon in any direction you may choose. Once you have crossed that horizon you may have physically disappeared from your old life and world, but you still exist. You just don't exist where you once did. People's fear of me stems from the fact that they don't know what is over the horizon and if there is life over there too, which, of course, there is.*"

Me: "*So what about a real physical death? Do the same principles still apply?*"

Death: "*Absolutely! However, with physical death there comes a greater command to forget. But either way, old lives fade from memory like past dreams and people become consumed by the new life that consumes their attention.*"

Me: You're telling me that when I die a physical death, where I go will depend on the direction I am going when I die?"

Death: "*Exactly.*"

Me: "*What about the concepts of heaven and hell?*"

Death: "*Where you end up when you die is where you were going while lived. Your direction also depends on the Inorganics you choose as your allies along the way. If you believe in and feed your energy to Inorganics such as Hating, Cheating, Stealing, Lying, Conniving, Indulging, Killing, Warring, Marrying, Divorcing, etc., you will go to a world very much like this one. Would you call this world Heaven? Or, is it more like Hell?*"

Me: "*So picking one's allies is another way of picking a direction and world.*"

Death: "*It is the way to maintain a new direction. If you want to live in the world of a lean man, then Indulgence would not make a good companion.*"

Me: "*And if you want to live in a world where people accept you as you are, then Jealousy and Ownership wouldn't make great companions either.*"

Death: "Heaven and Hell are concepts created by people thousands of years ago as a way to explain a choice of direction and allies. But whatever your attachments are, you can bet they will determine where you will go."

"Eternity has nothing to do with the hereafter…This is it…
If you don't get it here, you won't get it anywhere.
The experience of eternity right here and now is the function of life.
Heaven is not the place to have the experience;
here's the place to have the experience."
~ Joseph Campbell ~

Me: "So why don't I remember the last physical life I had and the world I lived in?"

Death: "Why don't you remember where you were and what your family was doing all day the third Tuesday after you were born? When you are dreaming at night, why don't you remember that your body is asleep someplace and that you are only witnessing a dream? The unknown is a very difficult realm and topic for people, and something they would rather not consider. But if and when people decide that they would rather live in a world where they remember their entire existence and they actively decide to go in that direction, then memory becomes not only possible, but inevitable."

Me: "So the fact that people don't believe in such things is what keeps them trapped and unaware of the directional choices they are making?"

Death: "Of course. Unawareness is the direction they are going and therefore the product of the world in which they live."

"The fear of death is more to be dreaded than death itself."
~ Publilius Syrus ~

Me: "Fascinating."

Death: "The men you are trying to reach with your book will need to accept that there are other possibilities for relationships, especially the kind of relationships they most want to achieve. Their decision to go for those kinds of relationships will change their direction automatically and will align them with the world and future they most desire."

Me: "Most people are really anchored in the world they know best, though."

Death: "Of course they are. As I said before, they are attached to the known and this keeps them from dealing with too many surprises. You use your extra weight to keep yourself anchored in the world you know best. In your world, you can ignore wise nutrition more than you should and you can eat more food than you really should. You already know how people are going to respond to you, especially women, and you don't have to exercise as often as you should."

Me: "Okay, okay, I hear you. (I was starting to feel self-conscious and a little annoyed.) But I was thinking more in terms of anchoring one's self in unhealthy relationship patterns."

Death: "You mean not taking appropriate care of your body can easily create healthy relationship patterns?"

Me: "All right, all right. I see what you mean. But isn't the same true about men who constantly need to pursue unattainable women, and men who agree to terms they don't want to agree to, just because it is socially acceptable or politically correct?"

Death: "Most of the men on this planet would shit their pants and would run away like scared rabbits if they really got what they wanted. You did it yourself, remember?"

Me: "I don't remember that? I ran away because I got something I wanted?"

Death: "Remember that cute little blonde with the hot body you met at Bobby McGee's in Long Beach? You gave her your phone number and she called you up and invited you out for a drink at the Cannery in Newport, then took you home?"

Suddenly, the memory of this specific incident flooded my mind. It happened many years ago when I was in my mid to late twenties. I was trying to finish school at Long Beach State and was constantly daydreaming about meeting a good-looking woman who would stop all the cat and mouse nonsense and who would just give me what I wanted—what every guy wanted—and be happy to do so. I was taking a psychology of sex class at the time and was getting credit for writing papers about my personal experiences, so I was spending a lot of time at the discos trying to get as many personal experiences as I could. In those days, I spent a lot of time at discos anyway, but the class was added motivation because most of my fellow classmates were women, and we often had open discussions about our experiences in small groups or as an entire class. Although my female classmates often tried to verbally abuse and condemn me for my outlandish behavior, I loved to remind them that my behavior was always accompanied by a female who had behaved as outlandishly as me.

Anyway, I met this blonde one night who had a killer body. I bought her a drink and we hung out and visited until closing time. As we departed I wrote my number down on a napkin and handed it to her. I didn't wait for her to offer me her number and went on my way. I didn't expect to hear from her, but a couple of days later she called and asked me to meet her at the Cannery in Newport Beach for a drink after work. I really hadn't decided how interested I was by then, but I liked her willingness to call and solicit my company, so I went to meet her. We sat at the bar for about two hours sipping cocktails and telling our life stories when out of nowhere she suggested we leave and asked me to follow her home. The energy between us was good and I was truly enjoying her company, so I was instantly eager to grant her request. I couldn't believe my good fortune as I quickly finished my drink and escorted her out to the parking lot.

So far, I thought to myself while following her home, I haven't done anything but give this girl my phone number, and now she is taking me home. I was elated by the developments and I was experiencing a deep appreciation for my sudden stroke of good luck. I had been on a mission to find an attractive, straightforward, no-nonsense woman and it was appearing as if I finally had. She lived about fifteen minutes away from the restaurant, and by the time I walked in her house, I knew she had stepped right out of my fantasies and into my life. I swear that the front door wasn't even closed behind me yet when she started stripping me of my clothing. As she guided me across the living room she pulled my shirt off and was pulling my pants down as we entered the short hall to her bedroom. When I stepped across the threshold of her bedroom I also stepped out of my pants and my boxers, which stayed right where they were. I was completely naked by the time I reached her bed, except for my socks, and as I turned to face her she pushed me backwards onto her bed. She hesitated for a moment to make sure I was staying put, then she quickly pulled off all of her clothing and revealed her nice firm body and full round breasts. She pushed me again to make me lie down on my back, then she dropped to her knees and made me a very happy man.

I don't remember for sure how long we copulated in her bed, but as soon as we were finished with every position I loved, I was on my feet, gathering my clothing, and out the door in a flash. I jumped in my car and drove away as fast as I could without drawing too much attention to my late-night speed. As I drove home to Seal Beach, I felt a little panic and all I did was run nonsensical thoughts through my head about how this woman was probably trying to trap me and get me to marry her. I couldn't think of any other reason why she would be such a willing partner, a total pleasure, and so easy for me to have. And not once did it ever occur to me that the woman simply liked me and just wanted to enjoy my company.

It took about six months before I finally snapped out of my insanity and realized what a moron I had been. I actually discovered myself fantasizing one day about being with a woman who would behave exactly as the blonde had, and that is the moment when I finally realized what an idiot I was. I remembered the surprise look on her face as she sat in bed while I jumped up and ran out the door to my car. This woman had literally scared the shit out of me, and not because she was what I expected or even thought about. She scared me so badly because there was no way for her to know what I wanted, but she still exhibited nearly every single behavior I had recently coveted in my most intimate and private fantasies.

I couldn't phone her if I wanted to because I had run away before I ever got her number. I was too preoccupied with my thoughts while driving to and from her house to remember exactly where she lived. But who knows if I would have contacted her anyway. I was still shaking in my boots after all of that time.

"How many of our daydreams would darken into nightmares
if there seemed any danger of their coming true!"
~ Logan Pearsall Smith ~

Me: "I was one of those guys that preferred the pursuit over the catch. No matter how long it took me to catch someone, I would find something wrong with her after *I caught her so I could go pursue someone else*. Thank God I got over that one."

Death: "But the Richard who preferred the pursuit over the catch didn't die overnight, did he?"

Me: "It took me years to starve him to death, but I did and good riddance."

Death: "You're not the only man who's been scared of getting what he really wants. Men often hang onto their shit like it was gold."

Me: "Well, *maybe if it could be a swift death and we could just step over that threshold and find ourselves in a new world, it might be easier for us. It's that starving the old self to death that seems to get in our way.* Personally, if I could just stop eating like I stopped smoking, it would be easier for me, but I can't, because I have to eat."

Death: "That's what people think when they commit suicide; that it will all be over in a flash. But the only thing they accomplish is sending themselves to another world where they have forgotten everything, and where suicide is a viable option to life. Then, they still have to face all of the same hardships over again without the memory of their previous accomplishments. So you are better off changing directions from right where you are."

Me: "*There is no easy way out of our bad habits*, is there?"

Death: "The old self is self-important and sustains the world by growing thousands of tentacles that attach themselves to it. Through these tentacles, or fibers really, you exchange energy with the world and maintain it. And the only way to free yourself is to begin by severing them, one at a time, until you completely cut through them all. The old self will continue to whine, complain, and beg you not to cut through them, of course, because he knows it means his death."

Me: "So how do I keep from giving in?"

Death: "Stop feeling sorry for him. Stop feeling sorry and empathizing with a guy who keeps accepting conditions and demands from lovers that don't work for him. Stop feeling sorry for a guy who marries women that take his wealth and who shame him into guilt for acting and thinking like a guy."

Me: "You know, I was at a business recently working on a project in the conference room with a guy who is the owner. While we were working together one of his female employees walked in. She walked past me to the corner of the room where a bookshelf was and she squatted down and bent over to pull some materials out. While she was bent over another female employee walked in and asked us if we had seen the first woman who was bending over. Before we could answer her she noticed the woman bending over and said, 'Oh, there you are'. Then she laughed and told her fellow employee that she recognized her instantly from her backside. We all had a good laugh at this and then I spoke up and commented how my male companion and I would have been in deep trouble if we would have said something like that. The two women laughed again and acknowledged this truth. Then my male companion volunteered the information that even though we would never say it to them, we would recognize any of the fifty-plus female employees at that business by their backside. I chuckled to myself and thought how true his comment was, but one of the women turned to him and said, 'That's a shame'."

Death just looked at me with those dark piercing eyes for a moment.

Me: "My point is that the guy broke down and agreed with the women. I thought he did it just to defer any consequences his comment might evoke, but after they left the room he told me that it really was a shame that men notice and pay such close attention to women's body parts. I couldn't believe it! He was letting those women shame him for being a guy and for appreciating one of the wonderful things that make us men."

Death: "He has been living in a world where it has become popular to shame men for being men, and he is attached to it, buying in, and now sustaining it with his energy."

Me: "I was shocked! And I don't think he has a chance of escaping his remorse and shame for being guilty, simply by male association. What a way to live."

Death: "Well, there is another factor you have to consider."

Me: "What other factor? What do you mean?"

Death: "You have to take into account the body's memory and not just the implanted social mind."

Me: "How so?"

Death: "The body's memory conditions the physical body to crave the world it has been living in and to do everything it can to sustain it. So your business friend's body memory tells him to agree with those women who think a male's normal behavior and desires are a shame."

Me: "You're kidding! His body does that?"

Death: "Your body has memory, just like the brain does. Haven't you noticed that every time you lose twenty or thirty pounds your body always tries to go back to that weight? Even when you know you shouldn't be hungry your body sends you signals to get you to eat more, so you'll make your body go back to where it has been. It's like anything else that has shape. If you try to straighten out a piece of metal that has a bend in it, the metal will try to go back to being bent the way it was."

Me: "Damn, my body is working against me to keep me in the world of a fat guy?"

Death: "Not only that, it will try to keep you in any world you have become familiar with, because it is a neuro-chemical process. The hypothalamus, which is the lower portion of the human brain, kicks out a chemical your scientists call a 'peptide'. And these peptides are sent throughout the body and absorbed by your cells. Each cell in your body has receptors for these peptides, so the cell can catch and absorb them. When your hypothalamus sends out a certain peptide over and over, your cells create more receptors for that peptide each time the cell replicates itself. In your case, Richard, you have conditioned your body to love meat, potatoes, bread and butter, gravy, eggs, cheese, fatty Mexican food and fatty fried foods in general, so your hypothalamus sends out peptides related to this type of diet. The more you eat these foods the more often the related peptides are created by the hypothalamus and released into your system, and the more often your cells reproduce themselves with more and more receptors for these peptides and this diet. Eventually, you can see how every cell in your body demands that you continue to eat these foods, because they are so hooked on them."

Me: "No wonder I have never developed a taste for healthy foods like veggies. So this is true of moods and thoughts as well?"

Death: "If you have been depressed or even afraid of something over time, your hypothalamus has been sending out related peptides and your cells have become hooked, so your body demands that you give it depression and fear."

Me: "So the same would be true of becoming apologetic for being male?"

Death: "Of course it would. If you grow up with any belief system, your body becomes attached to that belief and demands that you continue it."

Me: "In other words, the body becomes addicted to the foreign installation of the social mind?"

Death: "The body becomes addicted to anything that it is subjected to over time, including drugs, exercise, foods, moods, attitudes, belief systems, etc."

Me: "So a person's physical body is literally working against his desire to change?"

Death: "It's way more than that. A person's physical body affects his thoughts and expectations at a powerful and subconscious level, and therefore has a great deal to do with creating his day, his future, and the world in which he lives."

Me: "So people who date, marry and divorce people who aren't good for them repeat this pattern over and over because their bodies are addicted to it?"

Death: "Their bodies are so addicted to it that they often feel what they call 'chemistry' when they meet one another."

Me: "Holy shit! I see it! Then we become addicted to the 'chemistry' and turn away those we don't seem to have any chemistry with? And then we continue to meet, date and marry the same people over and over because our bodies have such a powerful reaction to them. Wow, what a vicious cycle, and we try to tell ourselves that it's love."

Death: "Chemistry is physical recognition of something familiar."

Me: "This is why we tend to marry people just like our parents then? We are psychologically and physiologically conditioned to seek the type of love our parents and families practice while we were growing up."

Death: "When you meet a woman like dear old mom you have chemistry."

Me: "If love was abusive then we have chemistry with abusers?"

Death: "Or, you become the abuser and look for a punching bag to marry."

Me: "Well, I've certainly dated a large number of women like my mom."

Death: "Everyone does, even when it doesn't appear on the surface as if they are the same."

A number of past lovers ran through my head. On the surface, they appeared very different than my mother, because they had different looks, tastes, occupations and hobbies. But when I looked underneath all of these surface issues I could see very similar patterns of other attributes, like the levels of responsiveness, warmth, coolness, support, disappointment and expectation. So there was no doubt about it—I had dated and coupled up with my mother most of my adult life, even though the women had different names and faces. Then a recent conversation with a woman friend occurred to me. She had just rejected a guy because she said she "didn't feel any chemistry" with him.

Me: *"Ha! Women are always accusing men of thinking with our dicks, but that is exactly what they are doing too! They are thinking with their crotches and sex organs when they turn a guy away because they 'don't feel any chemistry' with him."*

Death: *True, but that doesn't mean they'll admit it or give the practice up. If they did they would have to face me en masse."*

Me: *"Most men look for that chemistry too, so it'll be a major shift in consciousness for them to do otherwise. Man, I am really seeing the enormity of the challenge this is going to be."*

Death: *"It can be done."*

Me: *"Well, I certainly believe that, but look at my business friend and how he apologized to those women for telling the truth. He really believes he has to apologize for being male and that he is automatically guilty of shameful thoughts and deeds just because he is a guy. His death will certainly be a major hurdle for him to overcome."*

Death: *"You may have noticed that every man eventually dies, one way or another, but few men ever really live."*

Me: *"I'm not sure there is any hope for him, or for many of the men who have bought into the shame of being male."*

Death: *"When men, or women, allow those parts of themselves to die that keep them from living in the world they usually dream about, they grow in personal power. By letting the shameful guy die, the fat guy die, or the jealous guy, the possessive guy, the insecure guy, etc., the power to choose one's destiny grows exponentially. In fact, it can grow so much that he can eventually choose the time and place of his own physical death."*

Me: *"People can actually choose the time and place of their death, without committing suicide?"*

Death: *"Absolutely. I stalk everyone, and men can change their minds about the direction of their lives at any point in time. If you look at any human being closely you can see my shadow directly behind him, always lurking there, just a couple of feet away, and always ready to serve."*

"A man who won't die for something is not fit to live."
~ Martin Luther King, Jr. ~

++

TO BE CONTINUED

++

ADDITIONAL RESOURCES AND THANKS

RICHARD'S WEB SITE

Please visit me at my web site *http://www.thebibleformen.com* to find out about the release of *The Bible For Men: Volume II*, the next book in this series. Or you can visit the website to e-mail me if you would like to share your thoughts about this book, or if you would like to share some of your own personal experiences. For obvious reasons, I cannot guarantee a personal response to every contact, but I would love to hear from you and get your feedback about anything that was helpful to you. I would especially like to hear about the experiences and dilemmas you encounter while attempting to follow the principles outlined in this book as well. I hope to take many of your comments and questions and use them anonymously in the followup volumes of *The Bible For Men* that are currently being written. The more feedback I get, the more I can address my recommendations to specific issues you are facing.

There are a host of excellent web sites that contain "personal ads" and that reach tens of thousands of people throughout the U.S. and the world. For example, I have helped to create a website called "RainbowBridges.us" with a female partner to provide my readers and the limitless members of each gender with matches that we specifically selected for them. It is a great place to learn secrets about one's self and to find out secrets about our potential matches and mates. Why wonder what to expect when much of the information we need can be provided up front? I personally like the idea of meeting highly diverse, accepting, and wonderful other-gender partners who are looking for partners like me. If they are nurturing caretakers or hard-nosed business executives, I would like to know how best to deal with them, and this site helps each member with this vital understanding. Whatever people's requirements are, it is highly likely we can match them here with someone who fits their needs.

For those who prefer to surf and find their own matches, I would recommend web sites like Match.com, the personals at Yahoo.com, AmericanSingles.com, Greatgirlfriends.com and Greatboyfriends.com, which are all fun. A Google.com search will reveal more personals' web sites than anyone will be able to use, so a look there would probably be wise. I personally like the Greatgirlfriends.com site because it was created by E. Jean Carroll and her sister Cande. E. Jean is a writer for *Elle* and the author of *Mr. Right; Right Now*, which is a great book for men to read because it was written as a six-week guide for women who wish to land highly desirable men in a relatively short amount of time. But have care when using Greatgirlfriends.com because there are a lot of powerful women there who are accustomed to having it their own way and who lure men into endless pursuits.

THANKS

A special thank you also needs to go out to several people who donated their quotes to this book, such as:

"And for power to come to you, you must make a place within yourself for that power to live."
Lynn V. Andrews
From: *The Women of the Wyrrd*

"When women hold off from marrying men, we call it independence. When men hold off from marrying women, we call it fear of commitment."
Dr. Warren Farrell
From: *Why Men Are the Way They Are*

"My days of whining and complaining about others have come to an end. Nothing is easier than fault finding... All it will do is discolor my personality so that none will want to associate with me. That was my old life. No more."
Og Mandino and wife Bette Mandino
From: *Greatest Salesman in the World Part II: The End of the Story*

"When men and women are able to respect and accept their differences then love has a chance to blossom."
Dr. John Gray
From: *Men Are From Mars; Women Are From Venus*

SUGGESTED READING

While you are you are following the recommendations of this book and patiently waiting for the release of my next edition, *The Bible for Men: Volume II*, here are some additional reading resources I would like to recommend. These books are a mix of psychological, philosophical and mythological works that will tantalize creativity and the imagination to no end.

1.
Robert Bly, http://www.robertbly.com
Iron John

2.
Dr. Warren Farrell, http://www.warrenfarrell.com
Why Men Are the Way They Are
Women Can't Hear What Men Don't Say

3.
Lynn V. Andrews, http://www.lynnandrews.com
Medicine Woman
Jaguar Woman
Dark Sister
Tree of Dreams: A Spirit Woman's Vision of Transition and Change

4.

Dr. John Gray, http://www.marsvenus.com
Men Are From Mars; Women Are From Venus

5.

Og Mandino, http://www.ogmandino.com
The Greatest Salesman in the World

6.

Dr. Herb Goldberg
The Hazards of Being Male: Surviving the Myth of Masculine Privilege
What Women Should Know About Men

7.

Carlos Castaneda
The Teachings of Don Juan; A Yaqui Way of Knowledge
Separate Reality
Journey To Ixtlan
Tales of Power
The Second Ring of Power
The Eagle's Gift
Fire from Within
Power of Silence
The Art Of Dreaming
The Active Side of Infinity

8.

Joseph Campbell
The Power of Myth (with Bill Moyers)
The Hero with a Thousand Faces
Myths to Live By

Printed in the United States
38605LVS00006B/46-48